22674A

GRANT G. GARD

CHAMPIONSHIP SELLING

Prentice-Hall, Inc. Englewood Cliffs, N.J.

Prentice-Hall International, Inc., *London*
Prentice-Hall of Australia, Pty. Ltd., *Sydney*
Prentice-Hall Canada, Inc., *Toronto*
Prentice-Hall of India Private Ltd., *New Delhi*
Prentice-Hall of Japan, Inc., *Tokyo*
Prentice-Hall of Southeast Asia Pte. Ltd., *Singapore*
Whitehall Books, Ltd., *Wellington, New Zealand*
Editora Prentice-Hall do Brasil, Ltda., *Rio de Janeiro*

Illustrations by Dean Fritz

Library of Congress Cataloging in Publication Data

Gard, Grant G.
  Championship selling.

  Includes index.
  1. Selling. I. Title.
HF5438.25.G37 1984   658.8′5   83-19115
ISBN 0-13-127530-5
ISBN 0-13-127522-4 {PBK}

This book is respectfully dedicated to my mother,

MYRTLE MAXINE GARD,

who has always been a true inspiration,
and to my son,

DAVID W. GARD,

who is an outstanding champion closer

CONTENTS

YOUR UNLIMITED OPPORTUNITY IN SELLING

We must have courage to bet on our ideas, to take the calculated risk, and to act. Everyday living requires courage if life is to be effective and bring happiness.
MAXWELL MALTZ

TOO MANY PEOPLE ARE THINKING OF SECURITY INSTEAD OF OPPORTU-NITY. As Arthur Brisbane said, "Some of us miss opportunity because we are too dull to try. Others let opportunity go by too much startled when they see it to take hold of it." Risk is always the price we pay for capitalizing on opportunities.

We hear much today about job security. I do not believe there is such a thing. If a person's only security is his or her job, and that person is laid off or the job is taken away somehow, then that person has lost everything, has been completely wiped out, and no longer has any security.

SECURITY MUST COME FROM INSIDE A PERSON. If it isn't there, it isn't anywhere. Security comes to people who are confident that they can handle any job of their choosing or that they can take command of any situation that challenges them. If they lose their present job, they know deep down inside that they can maintain their lifestyle by taking advantage of other opportunities or by boldly going out and creating new opportunities.

Selling is a proud profession. To the secure person it presents many opportunities every day that are virtually unlimited. The surest way to miss success is to miss the opportunity.

Champion closers look at every selling interview as an opportunity. They make new opportunities every day by smoothly and persuasively working with people and setting up selling interviews. After they have *made* their opportunity by setting up the sales interview, they then *capitalize* on that opportunity by successfully closing the sale. Champion closers do not stand by and wait for opportunities to come to them. They make their opportunities. They always keep things moving and make favorable things happen every day. That's security. That's self-confidence in positive action.

I firmly believe the purpose of education is not just to accumulate knowledge. True education should show people how to use their knowledge successfully to achieve their goals. The question never has been and never will be how much a person knows. That can be determined easily. The real question is what use can a person make of what he or she knows. It's possible, and it is being done today by many people, to have all kinds of knowledge and education and still "flunk out" in the sales and/or business world. The important part of knowledge is being able to use it when working with people and situations to obtain desired results. Knowledge by itself is not power. Application of knowledge and education to achieve positive results is power. Positive application of knowledge and education creates *inner security* and *opportunities.*

YOU CAN BE EITHER A CREATURE OF CIRCUMSTANCES OR A CREATOR OF CIRCUMSTANCES. In the free enterprise system every individual is given an opportunity to *compete* or *create.* If you choose just to compete with everyone in the selling profession and handle your job with the same level of competency, then you must be satisfied with the same income, the same rewards they are receiving. But why settle for that? Why not chose to be outstanding, and join the select few who consistently create opportunities and who are creators of circumstances? You'll not only develop much more *real* security, but the rewards will always balance out, and you'll quickly find yourself in the select upper-income bracket.

The sales ideas in this book come from more than twenty-five years of successful personal selling and training experience. I do not claim to have all the answers. No one ever will. Through trial and error I have found some simple, basic, proven sales ideas that I will share with you in this book. I'm confident they will help you make even more opportunities and capitalize on your opportunities.

OPPORTUNITY FOR DISTINCTION LIES IN DOING ORDINARY, SIMPLE THINGS BUT DOING THEM VERY WELL. These are times when only your best will do. Successful salespeople who are in the select group of top producers in every organization achieve their job victories by doing the necessary, ordinary, simple things. But everything they do, every move they make, is done extremely well.

Several years ago I worked on Saturday mornings with groups of prisoners in the Colorado State Penitentiary at Canon City, hoping to give these people some skills and ideas that they could use on the "outside" to help them obtain and hold jobs. I'll never forget the time when I was talking to a prisoner who had served his time and was about to be released. He was an artist. I asked him what he was going to do when he was a free man. As he showed me a painting he had done of a beautiful, colorful, full-blooming plant, he said, "I've decided I want a job as a salesman. I want to prove that I can be the best there is. I figured it out, and in order for me to capitalize on any selling job opportunity I get, I've got to be just like this pretty plant. I've got to bloom wherever I'm planted." At the bottom of the painting were the words "Bloom—Wherever You Are Planted."

My purpose in writing this book is to give you a complete set of practical, simple selling tools to help you to be your best always, to be a secure, outstanding salesperson—a real champion closer who constantly creates and capitalizes on opportunities so that you can bloom wherever you are planted and truly be a creator of your positive circumstances!

Grant G. Gard

chapter one

CHAMPION CLOSERS USE THEIR FULL INNER RESOURCES

Men are often capable of greater things than they perform. They are sent into the world with bills of credit, and seldom draw to their full extent.
HORACE WALPOLE

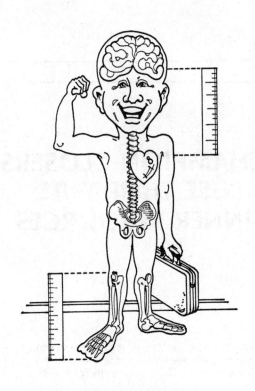

THE TWO 18-INCH LINES OF ACHIEVEMENT

WE ARE ALL RICHER THAN WE THINK WE ARE. Right now you have everything necessary to reach your selling goals. Your body is truly one great success machine, but like the farmer's ground and the soil around your house it doesn't care what you plant in it. Nor does it care how well you feed, water, or cultivate whatever it is that you planted in it. You will always harvest exactly what you have planted and cared for, no more or no less.

THE FIRST 18-INCH LINE OF ACHIEVEMENT. At the top of your body are two vital organs with great potential just waiting to be fueled. Fueling these organs in a positive manner with desire, determination, dedication, professional selling skills, sincerity, goals, integrity, honesty, true caring about the prospect, product knowledge, courage, motivation, organization, the right attitude, and enthusiasm can bring you to great heights of accomplishment.

Your *brain* is just lying there waiting for positive commands to get into positive action. Here's where you get the *logic* that goes into every selling situation. Eighteen inches down from the brain is the *heart*. Here's where you get the *emotion* that must be present in every selling experience. To sell what you know successfully involves both of these great sources of power, a balance of logic (brain) and emotion (heart).

If you supply a prospect with too much logic and not enough emotion, you have a very well-educated prospect but no *order*. If, on the other hand, you leave your prospect with too much emotion and not enough logic, you probably will make the sale, but the phone will ring the next day and you'll have a back-out, a case of "buyer's remorse."

THE SECOND 18-INCH LINE OF ACHIEVEMENT. A professional salesperson loves to sell. The pro knows that selling is first rate. The pro realizes that selling is not an occupation that should be looked down upon. Professionals aren't ashamed of working, selling, calling on prospects and customers. They are ashamed only when they *aren't* working.

YOU CAN'T MAKE A SALE IF YOU DON'T MAKE A CALL. Nothing good happens unless you get into positive action to make it happen. Therefore, the second 18-inch line of selling success runs from the *knee* to the bottom of your *foot*. You must work and work smartly, be ambitious, energetic, on the move, making every minute of the day productive and paying maximum dividends. I always admire salespeople who wear out the soles of their shoes. They've been out in the world of prospects and have been making things happen and keeping things moving.

FOUR TYPES OF BONES

EVERY ORGANIZATION IS MADE UP OF FOUR TYPES OF BONES. First there are the *wishbones*. They stand around wishing for great things to happen, but they don't get into action to make it happen. Then there are the *jawbones*. They do a lot of talking but produce very few results. Next come the *knucklebones*. They are busy using their time knocking everything and everybody. And finally there are the *backbones*. They are the action people who produce outstanding results. Champion closers are backbones.

   The reason why many salespeople do not succeed is that their wishbones, jawbones, and knucklebones are where their backbones ought to be.

SELLING WITHOUT WORKING?

I have a book in my library that is in very great demand. It has an intriguing title: *How to Sell Without Working*. When you open up the book, you find that every page is absolutely blank. Nothing has been printed on any page between the covers. Unfortunately, I know and you know many salespeople who are wishers. They wish they could get to the top; they wish they could make a lot of money; they wish they could get a promotion; they wish they could take an expensive vacation; they wish they could sell without working. Selling can do all of these things for you, but I know of *no* way to sell successfully without working. You cannot wish yourself into a successful selling career. You must hammer, work, and forge one for yourself.

CHAMPION CLOSERS USE THE BASICS

The two simple, basic 18-inch lines of achievement are all it takes to bring about the realization of your dreams—your worthy goals. The greatest and most powerful things in life are the simplest and most basic. Far too many salespeople today are trying to find a quick answer to their selling problems through a lot of psychological mumbo jumbo. But in reality success comes from understanding the basics of selling skills, product knowledge, and motivation, and applying those basics to people and situations to obtain desired results.

WHAT MAKES A CHAMPION CLOSER?

THE ABILITY TO KEEP THE SALE CLOSED. We all have seen the hot-shot salesperson who has one outstanding month or year and then tumbles, is washed out, and never regains momentum. We also have seen the flashy salesperson, perhaps the best-educated, best-dressed, and most charming. This salesperson makes a big flash on the scoreboard and then makes a big splash right into the water, never to regain high production, because of misrepresentation, high pressure, and deceptive tactics.

The super salesperson is the one who tells from the head and sells from the heart. His or her sales stay glued forever. This salesperson is steady, dependable, and well disciplined. This outstanding salesperson produces an above-average volume of business every year and has built the territory in order to have an above-average number of repeat customers who wouldn't think of buying from anyone else. The champion closers are a real contrast to the clever, flashy, deceptive, high-pressure salespeople who may produce outstanding results for a very short period of time but then fall off into low production and/or get out of the selling profession leaving a territory full of dissatisfied buyers behind them.

The one common denominator of champion closers is their

ability to keep their customers sold over a long period of time by inspiring complete customer loyalty. The champion closer keeps sales closed by using the right balance of logic and emotion, and he or she works hard to make good on every promise made to the customer.

CHAMPION CLOSERS ARE PEOPLE BUILDERS WHO REALIZE THAT THEY ARE IN THE PEOPLE BUSINESS. Customers will not put up with neglect for very long. Champion closers know that they aren't through with the customer when they leave with the order and check in hand. They know that they must turn this completed sale into a permanent customer. Each permanent customer can become a great source of additional future business. Champion closers build each sale into a permanent customer by staying in touch to find out how the customer is getting along with the product, if there are any questions, or if there is any way that they can help the customer to use the product successfully.

In this day and age there is no excuse for losing customers because of neglect and lack of follow-up on the part of the salesperson. Follow-up can be made in person, by a phone call, or by writing a letter. The sale is not really and truly closed until the customer has received the product and is benefiting from it.

Henry Ford's business creed said this: "The sale starts only when the order is signed. After that the duty of the seller is to see that the customer gets profit, satisfaction, advantage, and use out of what he has bought."

Champion closers never lose sight of the fact that they are in the people business and that their job in the end is building people and seeing to it that their product is used successfully.

Even though success in selling comes from the basics, let's see what is happening in the real world of selling.

EIGHTY PERCENT OF ALL SALES MADE ARE ACCIDENTAL

My work clearly shows that about 80 percent of the sales made in this country each year are made accidentally. Think of that! What do I mean by "accidental" selling? If you ask the salesperson why the sale was made, he or she can't tell you. If you ask why a sale was lost, the salesperson can't tell you.

One national company made a survey to find out how effective their advertising was. They sell a high-ticket product. They found out that about 66 percent of the people who walked through their doors had already made up their minds to make a purchase, either from that company or from a competitor. Management concluded, "All we have to do is train our salespeople not to talk them out of it," a terrible statement for management to have to make.

Over the years it has been reported to me many times by management that 20 percent of their salespeople are making 80 percent of the sales. That means that 80 percent of the salespeople are getting 20 percent of the sales, and that is not a very big piece of the action.

BE PROUD TO BE A SALESPERSON

SELLING—THE GREATEST OPPORTUNITY IN AMERICA. Sales is a great American specialty operating in the free enterprise system. It typifies the competitive spirit of the American economy. Nowhere else in the world have so many executives come up through the selling ranks.

SELLING IS UNLIMITED OPPORTUNITY AND POTENTIAL. It's all in how you handle it and what you make of it. I hear many salespeople make up excuses for not getting the sale—"I almost got her on the dotted line" or "I almost made that sale." In the demanding profession of selling, half sales don't count. Excuses are merely tranquilizers that some salespeople take when they do not successfully get the order.

Sometimes I hear, "When I've been in the business as long as Charlie, then I'll be able to sell like Charlie does." That is not true. Years in the selling business will not guarantee a person's success. I've seen many new people come into the selling business, and in three to six months, maybe a year, they are leading the sales organization in production. They are completely outproducing many of the old-timers who have been there for years. This is because they realize that a pro must be doing the right things right with the right people at the right time to obtain the right results. They are not complacent. They see the great potential and know the tremendous importance of growing with new ideas, new knowledge, and new skills to keep up with and capitalize on the opportunities of today.

THE PERSON WHO STOPS TRYING TO DO THINGS BETTER STOPS BEING GOOD. If you are not concerned about new knowledge and skills and are saying to yourself, "I have made a good living in the past, and I know all there is to know about selling," watch out! I know of *no* way you can let your mind rest on the complacency of past selling knowledge and victories and still be motivated to keep up with the fast-changing world we are living in. A complacent salesperson is like a freshly cut rose in a vase—looking pretty for a while but destined to wither and die.

YOU CAN REACH YOUR "SHOULD BE" POSITION
IN LIFE QUICKLY

Congratulations! The fact that you are reading this book is a sure signal that you are in the select group of salespeople who are headed for bigger and better things. You are receptive and are seeking new ideas to help you do an even better job in order to go from your "as is" position to your "should be" position in life as quickly as possible. I agree with Ray Hickok when he said, "You must keep everlastingly going to be a successful big game salesman. You ride the hunting grounds from early morning to dusk, getting your saddle sores and at times tearing your hands and face. But if you are well prepared in advance with good equipment, the right guides, hounds, and fighters ahead, you will get your share of kills at last."

ANALYZE IF YOU ARE GOING TO CAPITALIZE

CHAMPION CLOSERS ANALYZE. Self-analysis is a major key for growth. If you are going to capitalize on the great potential you have, if you are going to use what you've got to get what you want, you must make a good working habit of completely analyzing every interview, successful or not successful, in every selling day. Only when you analyze will you grow in the future. Otherwise you keep repeating the same mistakes time and again. One thing about the school of experience—it will repeat the same lesson if you flunk the first time. Build on your successes and learn from your failures. Unless you have complete knowledge of every phase needed in selling, you will not be able to sell analytically. You have nothing to compare your successes and failures to. It's possible for you to be doing the wrong things right and never progress.

ANALYSIS FOR SELLING SKILLS

Here are some key questions to ask yourself after every interview, whether the sale was made or not. All of these points will be covered later in various chapters of this book.

Did I make all conditions right to obtain desired results—the close? Did I see the right person who could make the decision? Did I plan for the interview as best I could?

Did I go in seeing myself making the sale successfully?

Did I open the prospect's mind and kill the words, "I'm not interested"?

Did I sell myself within one minute? Did I use the best human relations? Did I sincerely make the prospect feel important? Did I remember and use the prospect's name several times in the interview?

Did I ask the right questions? Was I a good listener? Did I interpret all answers correctly?

Did I find the primary interest and the dominant buying motive so that I could use motivational selling?

Did I build the prospect's confidence in me and overcome the three basic buyer's fears?

Did I give up too soon? Did I keep trying to close regardless of the no's I received?

Did I use empathy?

Did I keep the prospect's mind open and asking for more?

Did I use creativity throughout my sales talk? Did I oversell? Did I undersell? Did I follow every fact about my product with a related buyer's benefit? Did I successfully prove my claims? Did I use evidence properly? Did I use showmanship to prove my points? Were my examples clear and convincing? Was I brief and to the point?

Did I develop a real want by using my imagination to build a mind picture for the prospect so that he or she really visualized successful use of my product or service? Did I build up the value of my product to justify the price?

Did I use trial closes effectively? Did I listen and watch for closing signals?

Did I ask for the order at the right time?

Did I use the right close?

Did I effectively use concrete statements?

Did I have the right attitude about objections? Did I answer them effectively? Did I ask the right questions to find the genuine blocking objection? Did I use empathy mind conditioners? Did I know the type of objection the prospect had? Did I turn the objection into a benefit? Did I answer it at the right time?

Did I make my presentation move? Did I take too long getting into my presentation?

Did I have everything well organized? Did I look, act, and speak like a professional? Did I stay in control?

Exactly why did I make the sale? What did I learn from this experience?

Exactly why did I lose the sale? What could I have done to get the prospect on the right track? When and how could I get back to sell the prospect? What did I learn from this experience?

ANALYSIS FOR PERSONAL QUALITIES

Was I enthusiastic, a good listener, optimistic, courageous, animated, truthful, sincere, alert, loyal, well groomed, self-confident, tactful, positive in attitude, honest? Did I use good grammar? Was I self-disciplined? Did I display integrity? Did I have a good self-image? Was I punctual?

YOU CAN BUILD ADDITIONAL
SELF-CONFIDENCE

There is no doubt in my mind that self-analysis is the key to growth, additional confidence, and effectively selling what you know. As soon as you are away from the prospect, evaluate the interview. Be brief; time is valuable. If you don't have time, then be sure to evaluate at the close of each day. Make this a good working habit.

EACH TIME YOU ANALYZE YOUR FAILURES YOU WILL GROW, PROFIT BY YOUR MISTAKES, AND NOT MAKE THE SAME MISTAKE TWICE. Your selling ratio will improve, your time will pay bigger dividends, your attitude will be more positive, you'll enjoy selling even more, and you'll overcome a salesperson's fear of failure.

It takes a lot of serious, in-depth thought and foresight to look at yourself objectively. This can be done successfully only when you compare your experiences, positive or negative, to proven selling skills and techniques. One of the main differences between the amateur and the real pro is the way the pro analyzes interviews so that he or she can capitalize on every experience.

CHAMPION CLOSERS ADMIT WHEN THEY'VE
MADE A MISTAKE

YOUR ATTITUDE WILL DETERMINE YOUR ALTITUDE. A salesperson's success in every phase of selling is more dependent upon a positive mental attitude than on any other single factor. Look at finding and admitting your mistakes in a positive way. Look at asking for and accepting constructive help in a positive way. A negative attitude toward constructive help and criticism blocks growth.

Every salesperson I know has an off day once in a while, a day when things just don't go too well—no firm closings, appointment no-shows, and appointment cancellations. This usually results in a temporary loss of self-confidence. Depression sets in if the condition isn't corrected promptly. The pro turns this situation around quickly by having a positive attitude about finding and admitting a mistake and accepting constructive suggestions to get back on the right track.

When a star baseball player starts having off days, he realizes the tremendous importance in regaining his winning touch as quickly as possible. Self-analysis is started immediately. There might be just one small cause or it might be a combination of several things.

If the problem can't be located without help, the player asks the coach or an experienced professional to watch him in action to try to pinpoint the problem. When suggestions are made, he gladly accepts them instead of adopting the negative attitude so often displayed by less successful people.

THE MOST DIFFICULT SALESPEOPLE TO HELP ARE THE ONES WHO REFUSE TO ADMIT THEIR MISTAKES. They make up excuses for a poor showing and fail to put the blame where it should be—on themselves. They blame everybody and everything else. By resisting and resenting constructive criticism of a poor performance, the salesperson delays and very often permanently blocks growth.

Develop and consistently hold a positive attitude about yourself; about self-improvement; about your product, your company, your customers, your prospects; about constructive help and your career in selling.

YOU'LL BECOME AS GREAT AS YOU WANT TO BE

IT ALL DEPENDS ON YOU. There are many admirable potentials in every person. To become a dynamic, influential, top-notch salesperson, you must believe in the great potential you now possess. After twenty-five years of personal selling and training hundreds of salespeople, I believe strongly that no man or woman need conclude that he or she has to be a poor salesperson. That person may simply be uneducated or untrained. If that person really has a burning desire to improve as a salesperson and to close more sales, the necessary skills can be developed easily.

Webster defines *desire* as "an intense or strong craving." Your success as a salesperson will be in direct proportion to the amount of strong desire and intense craving you have to become a great champion closer.

William James said, "The greatest discovery of my generation is that human beings can alter their lives by altering their attitude of mind. If you only care enough for a result you will certainly obtain it."

Successful salespeople, the champion closers, come in all sizes and shapes. However, they all do have a common characteristic in their professional attitude—a strong, intense craving to close the sale every time they make a sales presentation. They feel nothing counts until the sale is closed. Closing the sale is winning. To close the sale is everything!

CHAMPION CLOSERS CRAVE TO BE GREAT

WHEN SALESPEOPLE ARE NO LONGER ANXIOUS TO DO BETTER THAN AVERAGE, THEY ARE DONE FOR. If you have the intense craving to be a great salesperson, you will become a great salesperson. Successful salespeople are not born; they are made great by education, training, and persistent development of their potentials to the fullest.

DON'T MISTRUST YOUR POWER

"The worst of poisons: To mistrust one's power," said Heinrich Heine. My experience in working with sales organizations clearly shows that around 80 percent of the salespeople are content with results far less than what they are capable of achieving. Many salespeople mistrust their power.

Read carefully what John Locke had to say about power over ourselves:

The most precious of all possessions is power over ourselves; power to withstand trial; to bear suffering, to front danger; power over pleasure and pain; power to follow our convictions, however resisted by menace and scorn; the power of calm reliance in scenes of darkness and storms. He that has not a mastery over his inclinations; he that knows not how to resist the importunity of present pleasure or pain, for the sake of what reason tells him is fit to be done, wants the true principle of virtue and industry, and is in danger of never being good for anything.

Just think of the additional business and income salespeople could develop if they had more desire, if they would set higher goals, if they would come alive, if they would not mistrust their great power, if they would quit dragging their feet, and would work with more spirit and energy; and if they would stop being content with anything less than achieving their worthy goals.

James Allen said, "Let a man radically alter his thoughts and he will be astonished at the rapid transformation it will effect in the material conditions of his life."

YOU HAVE UNLIMITED ENERGY JUST WAITING TO BE USED

People often ask me, "Where do you get your energy?" And we often hear remarks like, "I just don't understand where Mary gets all her energy." Arnold Bennett best explains energy:

Perhaps you've been hoping to create energy in yourself. Now, you cannot create energy in yourself or elsewhere. Nobody can. You can only set energy free, loosen it, transform it, direct it. An individual is born with a certain amount of energy, no more. And what is more important, you cannot put additional qualities into it. You may sometimes seem to be putting energy into him but you are not; you are simply setting this original energy free—applying a match to the coal or fanning the fire. Some people seem to lack energy when as a fact they are full of energy which is merely dormant, waiting for the match or waiting for direction. The usual idea of the amount of energy possessed by an individual is the intensity of the desire of that person. It is desire that uses energy. Strong desires generally betoken much energy—and they are definite desires. Without desire energy is rendered futile. Nobody will consume energy in action unless he desires to perform the action, either for itself or as a means to a desired end. You must not confuse vague, general aspiration with desire. A real desire is definite, concrete. Goals and strong desires set our innate energies free.

FURTHER DEVELOP WHAT YOU'VE GOT—YOU'LL GET WHAT YOU WANT

You've got everything it takes to get what you want. You must know, however, exactly what you want, the goals to be achieved, your "should be" position. You've got everything that makes up the two 18-inch lines of achievement. By further developing what you've got, you will move quickly from your present "as is" position to your future "should be" position and enjoy doing it.

MAXIMUM SALES RESULT FROM MAXIMUM EFFORT

Every year thousands of salespeople become frustrated and either quit the sales profession or are discharged. Why? Because they wish for maximum results but apply only minimum effort. They do not have the right spirit or a quest for excellence. Consequently, their sales production is much lower than the best results they are capable of. That salesperson is cheating himself or herself of the great rewards that come to a quality performer.

This poem was posted on the exploration ship, Quest, which was carrying her crew to the Antarctic.

If you can dream and not make dreams your master;
If you can think and not make thoughts your aim;
If you can meet with triumph and disaster;
And treat those two imposters just the same;

If you can force your heart, and nerve, and sinew
To serve your turn long after they are gone;
And so hold on when there is nothing in you
Except the will which says to them, "Hold on."

> If you can fill the unforgiving minute
> With sixty seconds' worth of distance run,
> Yours is the earth and everything that's in it,
> And, what is more, you'll be a man, my son.

The author of those spirited words is unknown to me but historical records point out that Sir Ernest Shackleton, who headed the exploration crew, named this poem "The Spirit of the Quest."

I urge you to apply maximum effort to every selling situation. To win in sales is everything. Do everything with a spirit and quest for excellence. Don't accept anything less. Make it a habit to work by "The Spirit of the Quest." You'll quickly become a quality performer and a genuine champion closer.

THOUGHT-PROVOKING QUOTES

Self-reliance and self-respect are about as valuable commodities as we can carry in our pack through life.
LUTHER BURBANK

Success is never found.
Failure is never fatal.
Courage is the only thing.
WINSTON CHURCHILL

You can dream, create, design, and build the most wonderful place in the world, but it requires people to make the dream a reality.
WALT DISNEY

The secret of success in life is for a man to be ready for his opportunity when it comes.
BENJAMIN DISRAELI

The trouble with most people is that they think with their hopes or fears or wishes rather than with their minds.
WILL DURANT

If you think you can or can't you are right.
HENRY FORD

The first step in self-improvement is to admit our faults.
ARNOLD GLASOW

Get happiness out of your work or you may never know what happiness is.
ELBERT HUBBARD

Most ignorance is vincible ignorance. We don't know because we don't want to know.
ALDOUS HUXLEY

The force of habit can take luster away from the best of pleasures. But habit can also create new and special pleasures in return.
HANS MARGOLIUS

We rest by changing the character of our work.
SAUNDERS NORVELL

I always try to tell them that it's what you learn after you know it all that really counts.
HARRY S TRUMAN

Professionalism is knowing how to do it, when to do it, and doing it.
FRANK TYGER

Tolerate imperfection in others, never in yourself.
FRANK TYGER

chapter two

CHAMPION CLOSERS ARE POSITIVE, COURAGEOUS, AND ENTHUSIASTIC

A coward flees backward, away from new things. A
man of courage flees forward, in the midst of
new things.
JACQUES MARITAIN

CHAMPION CLOSERS AREN'T AFRAID TO ASK THE PROSPECT FOR BUSINESS

A GREAT AMOUNT OF SALES TALENT IS LOST FOR WANT OF A COURAGEOUS, POSITIVE ATTITUDE. A courageous, positive attitude is vital for the success of salespeople. Webster defines *courage* as "the attitude of facing and dealing with anything recognized as dangerous, difficult, or painful, instead of withdrawing from it; the courage to do what one thinks is right." To see what is right and not to do it is just plain and simple want of courage.

One of the most successful salespeople I trained some fifteen years ago now lives in Denver. This man came into the sales profession after being a cabinet builder and carpenter. That was quite a switch. But he wasn't just a salesman. He was and is an outstanding salesman. In addition to being eager for sales know-how information, he was just as eager to take that information to the field and increase his "do-how." This man is now a leading real estate salesman in the Denver area. After observing him for several years, I have seen that he has many good sales qualities. They make him the champion closer that he is. But the one thing I admire most is that he never leaves the prospect without asking for his or her business. He is consistent and *always* asks for the order.

Like any other good selling technique, consistently asking for the order must be practiced at all times. It doesn't work to try it on one prospect today and then skip the next six or seven. To be a champion closer and to build a successful selling career, you must have a courageous, positive attitude and consistently ask every prospect for his or her business.

YOU CAN LEARN TO CONTROL FEAR

I am convinced that fear—lack of a courageous, positive attitude—will defeat many salespeople today just as it has in the past. We all have some fear, some nervousness, just prior to meeting a challenge or starting any event when we want top performance from ourselves. That's only human and natural. But to be successful in selling you must learn to control fear. Don't let fear control you. Go out and meet fear head on with a courageous, positive attitude, and you will soon find fear less dominant in your selling career and personal life. When you have learned to control fear and nervousness you will find that a little bit of fear and nervousness is good; it shows you want to do your best. It helps you get charged up for the interview. It gets your motor running. It gets you ready for positive action. Fear will be working *for* you instead of *against* you.

LACK OF A COURAGEOUS ATTITUDE
GUARANTEES FAILURE

Salespeople who lack a courageous attitude almost always have "excusitis." They make up excuses of all kinds for not doing the essential things required to produce sales. Problems and challenges become insurmountable obstacles. They give in to fearful, negative thoughts. They produce excuses, not sales.

To the person with the courageous attitude, problems and challenges are opportunities to grow and to show the world what he or she is capable of doing.

Never give in to fear. See yourself doing everything successfully. Successful people are willing to do what failures won't do.

Emerson said, "What a new face courage puts on everything. A determined man, by his very attitude and the tone of his voice, puts a stop to defeat and begins to conquer."

RISK IS THE PRICE YOU PAY FOR OPPORTUNITY. Many salespeople give up the selling profession because they refuse to risk defeat and/or rejection. They don't seem to realize that lack of courage always guarantees failure. They cheat themselves out of many great accomplishments and many great things they could have because they are afraid to try.

CONFIDENCE IS THE KEY. Two years ago my son David started in the selling profession by selling insurance. At first, door-to-door selling bothered him, but with his positive, courageous attitude he very quickly became master of the fear situation. At the end of three or four months, he actually enjoyed cold calling. He left that job for greater potential and started to sell securities for his own securities firm. Here again, fear was a factor. He had to make cold calls on the phone for appointments. He had to conduct tax shelter seminars for prospects. But after several successful experiences, fear has been overcome, and he now enjoys doing the things he used to fear. He is doing very well financially. He didn't give in to fear. He tackled and downed it with the right type of attitude and the bold conviction of courage. What he did, you also can do—*confidence* is the key. Successful experiences always build self-confidence.

Emerson also said, "He has not learned the lesson of life who does not every day surmount a fear. Fear always springs from ignorance. Men suffer all their life long under the foolish superstition that they can be cheated. But it is as impossible for a man to be cheated by anyone but himself as for a thing to be and not to be at the same time." True courage consists not in blindly overlooking danger but in seeing and conquering it.

ARE YOU MASTER OF YOUR FATE, CAPTAIN OF YOUR SOUL?

CONQUEST OF FEAR. A young man on a cot gazed at the brightness of the sun as it cut sharply across one corner of the room. After a while he turned and faced the wall. He had been in the Edinburgh infirmary for nearly two years while doctors tried desperately to save his one remaining foot. He had undergone at least twenty operations in the last twenty months. But he was not beaten yet. He turned and faced the sun again and smiled. Words rang through his mind, sang through his mind: "In the fell clutch of circumstance I have not winced nor cried aloud."

The man on the cot was William Ernest Henley. Few people in the world are called upon to endure as much as he had in his brief twenty-five years. He had suffered since childhood from a very serious tubercular infection of the bones for which the usual Victorian remedy was amputation. One foot already had been removed and the other one was threatened. It was in the hope of avoiding a second amputation that he had submitted to this long, lonely siege on a hospital cot. Doctors had a new method of treating infections, which they thought might save Henley's foot and keep him from becoming a complete cripple.

Fear, illness, poverty, pain, suffering, and endless treatments and operations had tested his courage to the limits. That had been Henley's life for almost as far back as he could remember.

"But I won't give up," he promised himself on the hospital cot. "I won't give up no matter what happens. I thank God for my unconquerable soul!" Out of the pain and suffering of his personal life, out of courage, faith, and fortitude with which he accepted the cruel blows of fate, came "Invictus," one of the most emotionally powerful and uplifting poems ever written.

> Out of the night that covers me,
>   Black as the Pit from pole to pole
> I thank whatever gods may be,
>   For my unconquerable soul.
>
> In the fell clutch of circumstance
>   I have not winced nor cried aloud.
> Under the bludgeonings of chance
>   My head is bloody but unbowed.
>
> Beyond this place of wrath and tears
>   Looms but the Horror of the shade
> And yet the menace of the years
>   Finds and shall find me unafraid.
>
> It matters not how strait the gate
>   How charged with punishments the scroll
> I am the master of my fate
>   I am the captain of my soul.

William Henley had tremendous courage, the same type of courage it takes in the profession of selling—to conquer fear and frustration, to make cold calls, to make appointments on the phone, to call on the "biggies," to make that next call after a turn-down.

THINK–ACT–TALK–LIVE SUCCESSFULLY

YOU MUST HAVE THE RIGHT ATTITUDE ABOUT YOURSELF. Others see in us what we see in ourselves. To be a successful salesperson you cannot dislike yourself and/or your profession. You must think you are important. You must know you have what it takes to be a top-notch salesperson. You must think and believe that selling is the greatest of all professions. You must think you can close sales successfully. The key to success is thinking positively about yourself. People judge you by your actions and your actions are controlled by your thoughts.

MAKE USE OF AFFIRMATION. Get rid of negative thoughts. Sell yourself on yourself. Affirmation works wonders. I've seen it with thousands of salespeople. It upgrades your thinking because you are stressing the positives and successes, not the negatives and failures.

Build your short ten- to twenty-second *pep talks* on four or five of your best qualities and capabilities. For example: "I've got first-rate ability"; "I'll bring my prospect the best money-saving equipment she has ever had"; "I'm enthusiastic about myself and my product, and I'll let it show"; "I'll help my prospect to prosper"; "I'll close this sale successfully"; "With my positive attitude I can handle any situation that comes up."

As a means of controlling your mind and making yourself do and believe the things you want to do and believe, nothing can touch the good working habit of affirmation and/or pep talks. This practice helps you to build and achieve higher goals. Give yourself several pep talks a day—when you get up, on your way to work, before the start of every sales interview, right after the interview, before you start any major event, just before you retire at night, and any time you feel down.

I know from training salespeople that some people feel this is something to laugh at, to make fun of, something ridiculous. This group of average thinkers simply refuses to believe that successes come from planned, managed thinking. Affirm the things you want to do and believe. When you repeat a thing often enough it takes over your mind. Soon it will become a reality.

A SALESPERSON IS HAPPIEST AND MOST SUCCESSFUL WHEN FULLY DEDICATED TO THE CAUSE

YOU MUST HAVE THE RIGHT ATTITUDE TOWARD YOUR PRODUCT. It's important to have a strong, dedicated, sincere belief in your product. Products should be sold with a professional spirit. The professional spirit comes from a real deep-seated feeling of the highest integrity and the greatest pride every time you make a sale. You know you have made a lifetime customer or friend because your product will perform and the buyer will receive more than his or her money's worth.

ENTHUSIASM IS AT THE BOTTOM OF ALL SUCCESS

YOU CAN AROUSE YOUR ENTHUSIASM AND KEEP IT AROUSED. Far too many salespeople are dependent upon someone—spouse, sales manager, other salespeople—to arouse and supply the enthusiasm needed to sell successfully. Basically, I have found that salespeople can arouse their own enthusiasm by (1) knowing everything there is to know about the product, that it's made the best and is of high quality, and (2) being confident that their product will greatly benefit the buyer. Your first-class product and the many product benefits it provides the buyer should set you on fire with enthusiasm. Enthusiasm sells! It sells you, and it sells your product. If you aren't honestly and sincerely excited about your product and the benefits it brings to the user, stop selling immediately! You'll never be very successful as a salesperson. A salesperson without enthusiasm is just an order taker.

> A salesperson not fired with enthusiasm
> Will be fired with enthusiasm.
> The Management

Don't delay—start right now developing a greater glow of inner excitement. Here's another great opportunity to use positive affirmation and pep talks. I'm not talking about shouting, yelling at the top of your voice, or waving your arms frantically and jumping up and down. I'm talking about a genuine, sincere, dedicated belief in the product you sell and a red-hot burning desire to transmit this feeling to your prospect so that he or she can enjoy the benefits. The salesperson who is excited is the one who sells. Enthusiasm is the greatest power you have to move you on to greater accomplishment. You must have it before you can give it, but when you've got it everyone around you also has it. Enthusiasm is contagious.

EXCITEMENT IS TO A PROFESSIONAL
SALESPERSON WHAT WATER IS TO A FISH

ENTHUSIASM IS THE BEST PROTECTION YOU HAVE TO CLOSE THE SALE. Wholeheartedness is contagious. The worst thing that can happen to a salesperson is to lose his or her enthusiasm for selling. Sales plunge immediately.

DON'T BECOME STALE. Every one of us has had the experience of going into a store when we had pretty well made a decision to make a certain purchase. We left the store without buying anything because of the dull, unenthusiastic manner the salesperson used when talking to us.

The more frequently you tell your sales story, the more easily you become bored with the whole thing. The sales talk becomes a canned, noninteresting group of sentences that completely lack color, excitement, enthusiasm, and persuasion—the qualities that make people want to buy.

The best way to keep from becoming stale is to remind yourself of the many benefits your product will bring to the prospect and that you want the prospect to remember you as a salesperson who sincerely wants to help the customer.

YOU MUST HAVE THE RIGHT ATTITUDE TOWARD PEOPLE. Your progress in selling will depend on your sincere interest in and your ability to serve other people. Working with all types of people successfully is another big challenge you face. Every person has to be dealt with individually. There are no carbon copies. You can't sell in a vacuum, and you can't sell anything without people. Every person is different and deserves to be treated as someone special.

You must convince yourself and genuinely adopt the attitude of liking other people and seeing them as important. You must sincerely have the "I care about you" attitude. That attitude will automatically get across to people without you even trying. Gimmicks and false ego massages won't work. You can't make the other person feel important if, deep down inside, you feel they are nobodies.

The important thing to remember is this: Your own attitude is reflected back to you from the other person. You control the actions and attitudes of other people by your own actions and attitudes.

Will Rogers said, "I never met a man I didn't like." That was one of the qualities he possessed that made him such a famous and great person.

Make a list of the most successful salespeople you know. Analyze their success. I'll bet everyone on your list has the ability to work smoothly and influence people. I'll also bet that the qualities of enthusiasm, strong belief in their product, and a good attitude toward themselves and others are also prevalent.

OTHERS ARE NOT GOING TO CARE ABOUT YOU UNTIL THEY FIRST KNOW HOW MUCH YOU REALLY CARE ABOUT THEM. Why should people be interested in you unless you are first interested in them?

Alfred Adler, psychologist and author of the book *What Life Should Mean to You*, said, "It is the individual who is not interested in his fellow men who has the greatest difficulties in life and provides the greatest injury to others. It is from among such individuals that all human failures spring."

Unfortunately, the world is full of self-seeking, selfish salespeople. Forget your commission check and just think in terms of helping people. The rewards will follow. It's the salesperson who unselfishly tries to serve others who has a tremendous advantage. He or she has practically no competition. Owen D. Young said, "The man who can put himself in the place of other men, who can understand the workings of their minds, need never worry about what the future has in store for him."

Champion closers are positive about themselves, their products, and other people. They are courageous and enthusiastic. They consistently display these characteristics, and they are very successful in producing desirable results—getting the order.

The biggest misconception about successful salespeople is that many feel they are super brains and that they are smarter than other people. The more you enjoy people and realize how important people are to your success, the more deeply you will look at people and realize that your challenge is to create ways to best sell yourself and creatively come up with ideas and the proper motivation to influence each person to buy from you. The right attitude toward people could be defined as your sincere interest in and your ability to serve other people. Your attitude and ability must be developed to the fullest.

To sum up, champion closers aren't afraid to ask the prospect for business. They are positive, courageous, and enthusiastic.

THOUGHT-PROVOKING QUOTES

Self-interest is but the survival of the animal in us. Humanity only begins for man with self-surrender.
HENRI FRÉDÉRIC AMIEL

The great need for anyone in authority is courage.
ALISTAIR COOKE

Unless a capacity for thinking be accompanied by a capacity for action, a superior mind exists in torture.
BENEDETTO CROCE

The spending of our energies is the greatest possible stimulus to their re-creation.
CHARLES DARWIN

Unless there be correct thought, there cannot be any action, and when there is correct thought, right action will follow.
HENRY GEORGE

You give but little when you give of your possessions. It is when you give of yourself that you truly give.
KAHLIL GIBRAN

Enthusiasm is self-generated pressure in the tank. Little is accomplished without it.
ARNOLD GLASOW

To do a common thing uncommonly well brings success.
HENRY J. HEINZ

Let no feeling of discouragement prey upon you, and in the end you are sure to succeed.

ABRAHAM LINCOLN

A sunny disposition is the very soul of success, enabling a man to do double the labor he could without it, and to do it with half the physical and mental exhaustion.

WILLIAM MATHEWS

Real unselfishness consists in sharing the interests of others.

GEORGE SANTAYANA

Blessed is the person who sees the need, recognizes the responsibility, and actively becomes the answer.

WILLIAM ARTHUR WARD

Within us all there are wells of thought and dynamos of energy which are not suspected until emergencies arise.

THOMAS J. WATSON

All things come to him who waits—provided he knows what he is waiting for.

WOODROW WILSON

chapter three

TWENTY-FIVE POINTS THAT EARN YOU A PROFESSIONAL SELLING IMAGE

A man's success in business today turns upon his
power of getting people to believe he has something
that they want.
GERALD STANLEY LEE

PROJECT A PROFESSIONAL IMAGE AND EARN
PEOPLE LOYALTY

YOU CAN'T BEG, BORROW, STEAL, OR BUY PEOPLE LOYALTY AND A PRO-
FESSIONAL IMAGE—YOU HAVE TO EARN THEM!! You earn them by leaving the people you have worked with so that they respect you, trust
you, like you, and admire you. Always be your best when you are
making your initial contact—or any contact—with the prospect.
Here are twenty-five key points to help you earn a professional
image and open the prospect's mind, thus helping you earn the
prospect's loyalty and close the sale. These points are as important
as the actual wording of your mind-opening statements, which will
be covered in chapter 5. These points are in addition, of course, to
the items covered in chapters 1 and 2.

1. TREAT EVERY INTERVIEW AS A VERY IMPORTANT MATTER. If you
   don't, the prospect won't either.
2. MAKE ALL CONDITIONS RIGHT TO PRODUCE YOUR DESIRED RESULTS.
   Make sure no one else is present except the prospect or prospects. Also make sure all interested, decision-making people are
   present. Everyone present should be comfortable and seated.
   Under no condition should you give any part of your sales
   presentation in the front office, the hall, or the doorstep. Your
   mind opener will get you into an office or home. That's the
   purpose. Make it a firm rule never to get involved in a selling
   situation until all conditions are right. If all conditions are not
   right, the odds are you won't leave with the order, so why risk it?
3. KNOW AND PRONOUNCE CORRECTLY THE NAMES OF ALL PRESENT.
   Everyone likes to be recognized and made to feel important.
   Everyone likes the sound of his or her name. It's the mark of a pro
   to call people by name. It helps to create the right type of atmosphere. Make sure you get it right the first time. If you don't hear
   it clearly, then ask to have it repeated or even spelled. That
   shows you are truly interested.

4. DO NOT START TALKING ABOUT YOURSELF, YOUR LIKES, YOUR DIS-LIKES, YOUR OPINIONS, YOUR ACHIEVEMENTS, YOUR PROBLEMS, YOUR FAMILY. Your prospect doesn't care about you. The prospect cares only about himself or herself and the things that affect him or her. Talk only in terms of the prospect's interests.

5. DO NOT START BY APOLOGIZING FOR TAKING THE PROSPECT'S TIME. Under no circumstances should you apologize for taking the prospect's time. You know you have something that will really help the prospect. Therefore, the time will be well spent.

6. SINCERELY MAKE THE PROSPECT FEEL IMPORTANT. Never tell a prospect, "I just happened to be in your area, so I thought I would drop in." Whenever I am approached by a salesperson who uses that approach, I say to myself, "Gee, I must not be very important. He just thought as long as he was around the area he'd gamble a few minutes, nothing better to do. He might find a live one." This type of thinking is totally against the laws of human nature. The deepest craving every human being has is to feel important, and that type of approach says the prospect is really not important. If you haven't got a good reason to make a call, then don't make it!

It is within your power to make other people feel important, to make them feel better about themselves, and to help increase their personal worth by thinking other people are important, by recognizing other people, and by paying them sincere compliments and courtesies.

No two people are the same. People live differently, dress differently, work differently, and eat differently, but we all have one common quality: we all want and need other people to help us confirm our sense of personal worth. We want people to recognize us and make us feel important.

It costs so little to do this, and yet it means so much to other people. Making good working habits of consistently paying honest appreciation, compliments, and courtesies is the most effective and quickest way to improve yourself in human relations. I have always been very impressed with the way George Dana Boardman describes *habit:* "Sow an act, and you reap a habit; sow a habit, and you reap a character; sow a character, and you reap a destiny."

Don't underestimate your power of dealing with people effectively and working with people smoothly. Don't underestimate the power of this human relations principle of sincerely making people feel important.

7. DON'T START BY SELLING THE PRODUCT. SELL THE USE OF IT. If you sell the product itself you are dead from the start. G. Lynn Sumner said, "The most important development of modern selling is recognition of the value of selling not the article itself but the use of it. The seller must know everything possible about the use of the article in order to sell all its uses to the best advantage."

At the early stage of the interview, you are trying to get the prospect's undivided attention. Keep your mind on your immediate goal—to open the prospect's mind. This will never be a problem if you keep in mind that nobody wants the product. Prospects want only what the product will do for them, the benefits of the product. Talk *benefits* only.

8. MAKE EVERY MOVE PROFESSIONAL. Have a professional attitude. The way you walk, talk, sit, and act will have an immediate impact on the prospect. Be relaxed, act confident, talk like a success, sit up straight in the chair. Use just enough small talk or general talk to build a relaxed rapport and to break down any barrier between you and the prospect. Sum up the prospect during your small-talk period. The prospect will surely be summing you up! Here again your sense of timing is vital. Stay in control of the small-talk period. Too much time on this will kill your chances for a sale. The prospect will form an image of you as being a time waster, become aggravated, and stop the interview. On the other hand, you may lose the chance for a sale because you spent too little time with small talk; thus you did not build a friendly, warm, relaxed atmosphere in which the salesperson–prospect ice barrier was broken.

9. BE OBSERVANT. This is as important as being a good listener. Many times there are clues all around the office or home that will give you ideas that might assist you in talking the prospect's language and thus making the sale. Look for trophies, pictures, books, decor, awards, and plaques. It's a pretty safe bet that the prospect is very proud of anything that is on display in the office

or home, and if properly asked the prospect will gladly talk about some of those things.

10. DRESS FOR SUCCESS. You can't make a strong opening or a strong closing wearing a dirty shirt and a wrinkled suit or dress. Personal appearance is very important. I've always felt that a salesperson should dress about the same as his or her best prospects. Look like a person worth listening to. You want the prospect to respect you, so buy the top-of-the-line conservative dresses and suits, clothes that will hold up well all day long. The prospect you call on at the close of the day is as important as the first prospect of the day.

Appearance not only has an effect upon the prospect, but it also has a tremendous effect upon the salesperson. Good clothes and good grooming build your confidence and make you feel good. Your attitude is stronger and better. Deep down inside you know that you are so well groomed and well dressed that you would feel comfortable talking to the highest-caliber prospect in the world. That's a good feeling. You must earn your good first impression. Good-quality, conservative clothing and being well groomed are essential in building your favorable image.

11. HAVE FUN AND ENJOY YOURSELF. Create a positive selling climate by being cheerful and pleasant. Talk only about good news. The prospect will have an enjoyable experience. You will close many more sales.

Don't go face to face with the prospect and be the bearer of doom and gloom. Act happy and cheerful and you'll feel that way. Feelings always follow actions. Be the example of a person who loves the profession he or she is in and enjoys being around and working with people.

12. DON'T PEDDLE GOSSIP. Don't be a commercial visitor. Keep your mind on the purpose of the call. Salespeople go from prospect to prospect all day long and hear many stories, some of which may be true and some of which may not. Make it a hard and fast rule not to peddle gossip of any kind. You've got much better things to do with your time.

13. DON'T USE GIMMICKS OR DISTORT THE TRUTH. It's a shame to have to mention this, but it is going on today as much as it was twenty to

thirty years ago. Clever salespeople, instead of using their creative minds to create new, honest methods of opening minds and closing sales, spend a great amount of time creating gimmicks and distorting the truth in attempting to open the prospect's mind and make a fast sale. It doesn't work!

14. BE NATURAL. Use your personality to the fullest. Don't imitate others. Always insist on being yourself. You know you've got what it takes. All you have to do is develop and use your human relations abilities and selling skills to the fullest in your own individual way.

15. DON'T BE OVERANXIOUS. If you are too eager to make the sale, the prospect will sense this. Your role is that of a professional and knowledgeable counsel to the prospect. Never talk like a fast-buck salesperson who is anxious to make a deal.

16. LISTEN ATTENTIVELY. Bruyere said, "The great charm of conversation consists less in the display of one's own wit and intelligence than in the power to draw forth the resources of others." The only way to draw out and obtain the vital information necessary to close the sale is to ask questions properly. You must listen to the prospect very attentively if you are going to analyze and use this precious information properly to build your sales presentation. You do not have to do all of the talking to be a good conversationalist. Listening is the key to good conversation. Every time the prospect talks, it should be a learning experience for you. You are finding out what you will have to do to get the order. You can't learn when you do all of the talking. Some of my most embarrassing moments were the times when I was doing the talking when I should have been doing the listening.

Here are some suggestions for practicing the art of listening:

A. KEEP GOOD EYE CONTACT. Look at the prospect when he or she is talking. Tell yourself that the prospect is doing you a real favor by doing a great amount of the talking. It will help you to analyze what is being said.

B. DON'T INTERRUPT. To interrupt the prospect while he or she is talking is just plan bad manners. People are really complimented if you don't interrupt them until they are through. After a few interruptions the prospect probably will abort the interview. I know it's hard not to jump in and interrupt the prospect when the conversation turns to a subject on which you have a strong opinion, but use your self-control and strong will not to do it.

C. SHOW YOUR SINCERE INTEREST. To show your sincere interest, ask the prospect to repeat an important point one more time. "Would you please run over that last point one more time? It's so interesting and important that I want to make sure I understand it fully and correctly." Occasionally nod your head and smile.

D. PUT THE SPOTLIGHT ON THE PROSPECT. By focusing your total attention on the prospect, you are bound to get involved. Then something really good happens. You lose your self-consciousness. You will automatically become a better listener and a better salesperson. You'll keep in step with the prospect.

E. DON'T CHANGE THE PROSPECT'S SUBJECT. No matter how anxious you are to move on into the selling process, it is very dangerous to change the prospect's subject until you feel confident that he or she is through discussing that one point. Don't be known as a thought jumper, going from one thought to another without sufficiently discussing each point.

F. REPEAT AND QUOTE YOUR PROSPECT'S PHRASES TO GET YOUR SALES POINTS ACROSS. When the prospect has finished, repeat some of his or her phrases. "Mr. Smith, as you put it so well, . . ." or "Ms. Smith, I surely agree with you when you mentioned and so well expressed. . . ." It shows the prospect that you are a good listener. You are also paying the prospect a sincere compliment and making him or her feel very important.

Oliver Wendell Holmes was asked his advice on how to get elected to office. His reply was, "To be able to listen to others in a sympathetic and understanding manner is perhaps the most effective mechanism in the world for getting along with people and tying up their friendship for good. Too few people practice the magic of being a good listener."

Many sales are lost every day just because the salesperson did not realize the importance of properly opening the prospect's mind and finding out the prospect's needs, wants, and motives so that they can talk intelligently and build a strong sales presentation that will bring success. Yes, there's magic in being a good listener. The magic is that you will find out everything necessary to close the sale.

17. DON'T KNOCK YOUR COMPETITOR. There are no commissions paid for being a negative competitor knocker. Usually, it hurts you far more than it helps you. Don't fall into that trap.

18. USE *YOU* AND *YOUR*—DON'T USE *I WANT*. Again, the prospect doesn't care what you think, and he or she is not interested in you and what you want. Therefore, never use expressions like "I want to sell you," "I want you to listen to," or "I want fifteen minutes of your time." Forget *I want*. It will take practice, but it is well worth the effort. Your mind-opening ratio will go up with the more *you*'s and *your*'s you use.

Use *you* statements as much as possible. For example, "Your neighbor Mr. Jones asked me to call you," or "You will want to know more about this exciting blender," or "Don't you owe it to yourself and your family to give it one more try?" or "The fact that you are looking into this exciting opportunity certainly shows good judgment and wisdom on your part."

Insert some of these *you* phrases into your selling interviews:

"You will agree . . ."

"You will benefit by . . ."

"You know from experience that . . ."

"You have noticed how . . ."

"You feel, then, that model A is just right for you."

Here are five more *you* phrases that are quite effective:

The one most important word in the world is *you*.

The two most important words are *thank you*.

The three most important words are *if you please*.

The four most important words are *what is your opinion?*

The five most important words are *you can be proud of*.

Establish the good working habit of using *you* and *your* as much as possible and staying away from *I*.

It's always important to know what the prospect is thinking;

how he or she feels about your product, your new promotional idea, and so on. One of the best ways is to ask the prospect, "What is your opinion of this new type of promotion?" It's a big help because it gives you clues about what has to be done to close the sale, and it starts you talking and selling more from looking out of the prospect's eyes. Everyone likes to express an opinion. It makes him or her feel important.

19. USE EMPATHY, NOT SYMPATHY. Webster defines *empathy* as "the projection of one's own personality into the personality of another in order to understand him better." It is the ability to see things from another's point of view or to look out of another person's eyes. Empathy means you can put yourself in the other person's shoes.

Sympathy means, according to Webster, "sameness of feeling; a mutual liking or understanding arising from sameness of feeling." Empathy says, "I know how you feel, but I don't feel the same way." Sympathy says, "I feel as you feel."

When you use empathy in your selling you are seeing things out of the other person's eyes. You understand the prospect's position. You know and understand what has to be done to sell the prospect.

Many sales, however, are lost because the salesperson uses sympathy instead of empathy. When you get into sympathy with the prospect's objections and reasons for not buying, it means that the prospect is selling you rather than you selling the prospect. A sale is always made. Either you sell the prospect by using empathy or the prospect sells you by getting you to use sympathy. The more skilled you become at using empathy, the greater will be the service you can render your prospects.

20. DON'T ARGUE OR TELL THE PROSPECT HE OR SHE IS WRONG. A pretty sure way to have the interview aborted quickly is to approach the prospect with an arrogant attitude by saying he or she is wrong, and then saying you will prove it. That is no way to open a mind. You just hurt the prospect's pride and insult his or her judgment.

As Lord Chesterfield said to his son, "Be wiser than other people if you can; but do not tell them so." I hear so many salespeople say, "At least I had the satisfaction of straightening the prospect out and telling him a thing or two." What did the salesperson sell? Nothing.

Never tell the prospect you are going to prove something; just do it without using the word *prove*. By using this word, you're saying you are smarter than he or she is. The argument is on, and both you and the prospect must defend your positions.

I do not want you to misunderstand the point I am making. I am not saying that you should not get your point across. I know that professional selling involves turning the prospect around. That's the challenge of selling. There is a way to do it that will enable you to keep the prospect's good will and thus close the sale.

Why not use the empathetic approach? Whenever your prospect says something that you know is not right, start off like this: "Mr. Smith, I've been known to have made mistakes. I may be wrong. Let's take a minute and examine the record." Tactfully and diplomatically make your point. Let the prospect save face. Don't dwell on the error. Move on quickly to some other point.

21. THINK CREATIVELY. The whole selling process is an opportunity to use your creative mind, and you will be well paid for your creative efforts. Your creative mind is vitally important in building your mind-opening statement, creating ways your product will solve the prospect's problem, and mentally preparing your sales presentation. Be original with your mind-opening statements. Be different. Stay away from the old worn-out mind openers. Then, with the information you obtain, create a sales message that will sell!

There is no lock-in on creativity. It is not solely reserved for any particular group of people. You've been conditioned into believing that creativity is some kind of mysterious process, comprehensible solely to geniuses. That is absolutely not true.

Why do salespeople fail to use their creative faculties? It is easier to keep doing things the same old way. The sharp salesperson who uses creativity and imagination—green-light thinking, future-oriented—is going to far surpass the one who is complacent and uses red-light thinking, past-oriented.

Stewart said, "The faculty of imagination is the great spring of human activity, and the principal source of human improvement. As it delights in presenting to the mind scenes and characters more perfect than those we are acquainted with, it prevents us from ever being completely satisfied with our present condition or with our past attainments and engages us in the pursuit of some untried method."

Training your mind to become more creative is something that every salesperson can do. Are you creating or are you competing? Are you truly using your creative imagination to improve yourself, your selling skills and your closing ratio?

22. KEEP SALES MATERIALS AND EQUIPMENT LOOKING SHARP AND OR-GANIZED. The briefcase and any other sales aids and materials you carry into the interview make as much of an impression as your personal appearance and grooming. Keep all sales materials clean, neat, organized, and in top-notch condition. This is another factor in helping your selling efforts.

The tidiness of your sales equipment and materials reflects your attitude about your personal appearance and about being well organized in all phases of selling. Test all equipment to make sure it works before your interview. It is very embarrassing to have equipment failures in front of your prospect.

23. THINK THINGS THROUGH BEFORE YOU SPEAK. An idea, service, or product is only as good as you express it. Think things through. Make your oral communication brief, clear, and specific.

Dryden said, "We first make our habits and then our habits make us." The habit of speaking before thoroughly collecting their thoughts has cost salespeople many sales. Good communication will never come from a muddy mind.

24. MAKE EVERY CALL A SELLING CALL. I've heard many salespeople come out of an interview and say, "I just about got him on the dotted line. Came real close. I didn't make the sale, but I sure created a lot of good PR. We had a good visit." How much commission money did that call put into their bank account or their company's bank account? Not one cent!

Don't believe for one minute that the top-notch salesperson sees himself or herself strictly as a good-will ambassador, a contact person, or a missionary, and is satisfied by not making the sale. Know that your purpose on every call is to bring in the order.

Good PR is important, of course, but by itself it doesn't always produce sales. Therefore, make every call a selling call.

25. KEEP THE INTERVIEW MOVING. Keep the interview on the right track. Tactfully guide the prospects back on track if they stray off. There should be no dead time, no lulls, no stage waits. A good sense of timing is very important.

Using these twenty-five points effectively will help you to create a professional image and earn people loyalty, thus helping you to open prospects' minds and close more sales.

THOUGHT-PROVOKING QUOTES

To try and to fail is at least to learn; to fail to try is to suffer the inestimable loss of what might have been.
CHESTER BARNARD

A man is relieved and gay when he has put his heart into his work and done his best; but that he has done otherwise shall give him no peace.
RALPH WALDO EMERSON

Failure is only the opportunity to begin again, more intelligently.
HENRY FORD

Always take a job that is too big for you.
HARRY EMERSON FOSDICK

When a man is wrong and won't admit it, he always gets angry.
THOMAS HALIBURTON

Do not look back. It will neither give you back the past nor satisfy your daydreams. Your duty, your reward, your destiny are here and now.
DAG HAMMARSKJÖLD

It's amazing what ordinary people can do if they set out without preconceived notions.
CHARLES F. KETTERING

Life is not a problem to be solved, but a reality to be experienced.
SØREN KIERKEGAARD

Misfortunes are like knives, that either serve us or cut us, as we grasp them, by the blade or by the handle.
JAMES RUSSELL LOWELL

The world is not interested in the storms you encountered, but did you bring in the ship?
WILLIAM MCFEE

Quality is never an accident; it is always the result of intelligent effort.
JOHN RUSKIN

Our attitudes control our lives, attitudes are a secret power working twenty-four hours a day, for good or bad. It is of paramount importance that we know how to harness and control this great force.
CHARLES SIMMONS

Fortune knocks at every man's door once in a lifetime, but in a good many cases the man is in a neighboring saloon and does not hear her.
MARK TWAIN

Opportunity wears many disguises, including trouble.
FRANK TYGER

chapter four

HOW TO KEEP SALES TALKS FROM EARLY TERMINATION

They think too little who talk too much.
JOHN DRYDEN

TALK LESS—CLOSE MORE

AS EMPTY VESSELS MAKE THE LOUDEST SOUND, SO SALESPEOPLE WHO HAVE THE LEAST KNOWLEDGE ARE THE GREATEST BABBLERS. It has been proven to me many times that the knowledgeable salesperson talks less and closes more. Those salespeople who use the shotgun approach do very little planning, very little listening, and a great amount of talking. They scatter their many pellets over a wide area, hoping that one or two small ones will hit some kind of target that will warm up the prospect. They start selling the product instead of selling the related buyer's benefits of the product. They just know that if they tell the whole story enough times and see enough people the law of averages will take care of them. Ninety-five percent of the time they leave without the order . . . or they may get two orders: "Get out and stay out!" They blame the "stupid prospect" for their failure.

The pro salesperson uses the rifle approach, knowing that one well-aimed shot at the right target—the buyer's need, want, and motive—is all it takes to close the sale. They talk far less and sell far more.

BUILD YOUR CLOSING FOUNDATION EARLY

It is vital to have the proper attitude about yourself, your product, and other people. Here's a real opportunity to use your proper attitude by showing genuine interest in the prospect and figuring out a way to serve your prospect best. You need a closing foundation under the sale, and it is built right here, right now, before the selling interview starts. You must be able to speak the prospect's language. Most failures to close trace back to lack of understanding the prospect's needs, wants, or motives.

Failures don't realize that you can deliver your sales talk eloquently, have the best product, have a great amount of product knowledge, look good, be well dressed, be poised, feel your interview material was just what the prospect wanted to hear, have all of these things going for you and still not sell. You didn't get through to the prospect. You took a shortcut. You failed to build a closing foundation before the sales interview started. The target—the prospect's exact need, want, and motive—was never found.

Many salespeople play the guessing game, guessing at what the prospect's needs, wants, and motives might be. Guessing is a very dangerous thing to do and usually ends up with the prospect feeling valuable time is being wasted and terminating the interview very quickly.

HOW TO SELL CREATIVELY

MAKING AN ACCURATE SALES OUTLINE. Before any professional speaker gives a talk, the first determination is the exact purpose, the overall goal to be achieved. The speaker then prepares an outline of important points to bring that particular goal into reality; then he or she actually delivers the speech (the outline of points) with various speaking skills to bring about the successful achievement of the goal.

That basic format is also excellent for salespeople to use to build a strong closing foundation. In selling, the goal to be achieved, of course, is the close. To achieve that goal, it is necessary to prepare a tailored sales talk outline for each prospect, bringing in the points that will fulfill the particular need, want, and motive. Then the sales presentation is made according to the points in the outline using your best professional selling skills.

This is *creative selling*, and it will produce outstanding results—signed orders. Creative selling removes guesswork. Sell yourself on the importance of creative selling. No two buyers are the same. Each must be sold according to his or her particular situation. Salespeople who use strictly canned presentations are really hindered. The salesperson who is flexible and can use creativity and imagination in tailoring a sales talk outline for each prospect will be the one who has the highest closing ratio.

Creative selling has another advantage for the salesperson. It better enables you to analyze your successes and failures. This helps you to build your personal foundation of courage, confidence, and poise. This creates *positive momentum* in salespeople, and they cannot be stopped. Like the small snowball starting to roll down the side of a mountain, the further it rolls the bigger it gets and the faster it goes until finally it is unstoppable. Positive momentum creates one success upon another and makes the salesperson unstoppable.

THE TWO PARTS OF A SALE

A sale is divided into two parts. The first part consists of getting the vital presale information, building a closing foundation so an effective sales plan can be developed. The second part is the actual selling interview presenting the outlined material. The balance of this chapter will concentrate on the first part of a sale.

THE TWO TIMES TO GET PRESALE INFORMATION

There are two times to get vital presale information so that an intelligent presentation can be made. The first time is before you meet the prospect. In this case, it is called preapproach information. The second is the approach itself, which comes immediately after you have met the prospect and have opened the prospect's mind, but before you start your actual presentation.

1. GETTING VITAL PRESALE INFORMATION BEFORE MEETING WITH THE PROSPECT. When, how, and where can you get information about your prospect before you meet? What information is necessary?

   When? It may be minutes or hours, and then again it may be days, weeks, or months before you meet with the prospect.

   How? Very simply, as with the order, you have to ask for it. You must seek it out. Matthew 7:7 states, "Ask, and it shall be given you; seek, and ye shall find; knock, and it shall be opened unto you."

   What? Get all information necessary to build a creative sales talk from the approach to the close. How can you best serve the prospect? What is the need, want, and motive? What is the prospect's name (make sure it's correct) and title? How long has the prospect been on the job? When is the best time to see the prospect? Can the prospect make the decision? If not, who would the decision maker be? What product is the prospect using now? Is the prospect happy? What does the prospect like and dislike about the present product? What are the prospect's general interests—golf, charity, fishing, football? What are the prospect's accomplishments, personally and professionally?

Where? Get the information from the person who referred you to the prospect; from friends, associates, fellow church and service club members, professional organizations, and social workers; from local newspapers, radio stations, TV, phone books; from office receptionists; from general industry magazines and national, state, and local trade publications; from your personal observations around his or her office or home; from the Chamber of Commerce and the Better Business Bureau.

2. GETTING VITAL PRESALE INFORMATION AFTER YOU ARE FACE TO FACE WITH THE PROSPECT, AFTER OPENING THE PROSPECT'S MIND. Again, you ask for it. Assuming that you opened the prospect's mind on your approach (I'll cover ways to do that in the following chapter), I suggest you make a statement like this: "Ms. Smith, as I just mentioned, we have had a great amount of success in helping companies like yours in neighboring communities save up to 100 employee hours per week and still get the payroll out on time and with fewer errors, thus increasing their people's productivity and helping them to show more profit each quarter. With the thought in mind of determining what I can do or what I cannot do for you, do you mind if I ask you a few questions?"

ASK PERMISSION TO ASK QUESTIONS

Be sure you have the prospect's mind open. After skillfully asking permission, ask questions until you find out the *primary interest* and the *dominant buying motive*. If you have obtained a great amount of information before you meet with the prospect, open his or her mind and then through questions verify all of the information to be sure it is correct. Do not assume you have received correct information. Verify it. Get more information if you need it. That isn't hard to do when your heart is in the right place and you really care about other people.

It is necessary to ask questions until sufficient information is received. You must be clear in your mind about what the prospect needs and/or wants (the primary interest) and the reason why the prospect wants it (the dominant buying motive). Until you know those two things you are not in a position to sell anything. Don't leave it to chance. You must find the right road to the prospect's mind and heart.

SIX MAGIC WORDS TO CLOSE MORE SALES

Webster defines *motive* as, "some inner drive, impulse, intention, that causes a person to do something or act in a certain way." Knowing the prospect's dominant buying motive will help you increase your sales. Everyone has various inner motives. The key to successful closing is to find the one motive that is dominant in each prospect.

A product is not sold for the article itself. It is sold because it will do certain things for the prospect. Every product has an end use and an end result. Putting it another way, when you know what the prospect needs and/or wants you know the primary interest. To determine the dominant buying motive is really very simple, and here are the six magic words: "Why is this important to you?" The primary interest is what the prospect needs and/or wants. The dominant buying motive is why it is wanted.

Let's say that Mr. and Mrs. Smith are looking for a five-bedroom home that will give the right image for Mr. Smith when entertaining officials from the company who stay overnight there. Mr. Smith is trying to get a promotion in the company because he wants more salary and he wants stock options. The dominant buying motive is profit (greed, money). The salesperson who just sells a five-bedroom house is missing the boat. Mr. Smith is buying a promotion. The five-bedroom house is the primary interest, and the job promotion (more money, stock options) is why it is wanted—the dominant buying motive. All you have to do is say to Mr. Smith, "Why is a five-bedroom house important to you?" He will tell you his dominant buying motive.

In another example, Joe wants to buy a new 18-foot deluxe boat, fully equipped with every gadget possible. Joe's neighbor just bought a new boat that is outclassing Joe's present boat. Joe can't stand this, so he goes to the boat dealer and buys the best boat the dealer has.

Joe's primary interest is a new deluxe 18-foot boat. Joe's dominant buying motive is pride (prestige, desire for recognition). In Joe's mind, he sees the neighbors all standing around his beautiful boat and telling him how great it is, and Joe's pride is breaking out all over. That picture is exactly what was in his mind when he signed the order. If the salesperson asked Joe, "Why is this particular boat important to you?" Joe would tell him, "Well, frankly, I've always had a lot of pride about my boats, and my neighbor outdid me. I can't have that happen. I'll show my neighborhood what a first-class boat is really like."

There are many motives, some of which are fear of competition, the desire for power, fear of failure, pride, greed, envy, self-preservation, fear of poverty, love of family, pride of possession, fear of losing money or position, vanity, desire for peace of mind, love of ease and personal pleasure, money, desire to be recognized, desire for financial security, fear of criticism, desire for comfort, desire to be exclusive, desire to succeed. I could go on, but the main thing is that regardless of the number, all motives can be put into five categories.

THERE ARE FIVE MAJOR MOTIVES. Summing up all of the above motives and keeping it simple, concern yourself with five major motives:

Pride
Profit
Love
Fear
Self-preservation

ALWAYS SEEK OUT THE RIGHT DOMINANT MOTIVE. Memorize these five major motives. Determining which is the prospect's dominant buying motive is quite easy. One phrase does it. As soon as you know what the prospect needs and/or wants, the primary interest, then ask, "Why is this important to you?" and you'll find out why it is wanted. Creative selling to a strong motive will help you become an even better champion closer.

Whether you are *obtaining* information or *verifying* information, as was brought out in the last chapter, it is of great importance to tell the prospect the benefit he or she will receive from answering your questions. Keep it simple. Repeat your mind opener if you want. For example, "Ms. Smith, as I just mentioned, I have been very successful in helping businesspeople like you to reach out and get some new customers, increase their repeat customer ratio, and still cut their advertising budget. I might be able to do the same thing for you. With the thought in mind of determining what I can or cannot do, do you mind if I ask you a few questions?"

In another example, you could say, "Hi, Mrs. Jones, you sure know your cars. That model you are looking at is our newest and is the top of the line. We've been able to help many people save time, trouble and an unnecessary loss of money in solving their transportation problems. We might be able to do the same thing for you. With the thought in mind of determining what we can or cannot do, do you mind if I ask you a few questions?"

Give the benefits to your prospect first, why you want to ask questions, why they should want to supply the answers. Then you ask permission to ask questions. Unless the prospect really understands the benefits of answering your questions, he or she will balk, may even get angry, or will think you are just plain nosy. If you sincerely make it known that you just want to help, but first you must know facts about this particular situation in order to provide benefits, the prospect will work with you and give you the necessary information.

Recently a clever salesperson called me on the phone for an appointment. I granted the appointment. However, I was extremely doubtful about how sincere this salesperson really was. I very much dislike insincere telephone techniques, but I thought perhaps I'd go ahead and grant an appointment because I was interested in a phase of his so-called executive program. The salesperson arrived for the appointment and immediately began attacking me with direct personal questions. He failed to tell me why I should answer his questions, how I would benefit, and he talked in terms of his interest only. I felt I was being interrogated. His harsh way of asking questions really offended me. My doubts about this salesperson were correct. He was not genuine and sincere. I immediately terminated the interview.

You must do an effective job of selling yourself as a sincere and genuine salesperson.

My work shows that there are many salespeople today who could go from poor and medium producers to great and outstanding producers if they would build a closing foundation and get vital presale information before they started their presentations. They fail to get this information for various reasons. They are not sold on the importance of it; they are not self-disciplined with good working habits; perhaps some are in too big a hurry to get to the prospect and make the sale; some feel that they don't have the knack to get it from the prospect; some haven't been properly trained; some are afraid to ask for it; many salespeople feel they can sell without it; and some salespeople are just too lazy to work hard enough to get it.

STAY IN CONTROL BY ASKING QUESTIONS

AS YOUR QUESTION-ASKING TIME GOES UP, YOUR SELLING TIME GOES DOWN. Become a pro at asking questions. If you ask the right questions the right way, you'll get the right answers. Don't overlook the necessity of asking questions. You ask questions for the following reasons:

1. To create a professional image
2. To obtain information—need, want, and/or motive
3. So you can talk intelligently
4. To save time; to qualify
5. To verify information
6. To take a sincere interest in the prospect

7. To sell add-ons or related products
8. To close more quickly
9. To sell with empathy; to create a sales presentation that is tailored for a particular prospect
10. To make the prospect feel important

EMPATHIZE WITH BUYERS' MOTIVES

PLANNED, CREATIVE, MOTIVATIONAL SELLING IS FUN. It's also very profitable! People will buy from you because you are selling product benefits related to each prospect's needs, wants, and motives. You are looking out through the prospect's eyes. You are making it easy for the prospect to buy. You are making it logical for the prospect to buy. You are making it exciting for the prospect to buy from you. You're a pro. You found out what the prospect needed and/or wanted (primary interest) and why it was wanted (dominant buying motive). Prospects always like a salesperson who sincerely digs in and helps them solve a problem.

GOOD JUDGMENT ON YOUR PART IS CRITICAL

At the end of your information-seeking period, you should know the exact answers to the following questions:

Am I talking to the decision maker?

Does the prospect have authority to buy?

Does it appear the money is available?

What exact need for my product does the prospect have?

What does my prospect want?

What is the prospect's dominant buying motive?

YOU MUST ANALYZE YOUR INFORMATION QUICKLY AND MAKE A DECISION. You hope you are right. Your time is valuable and you can't afford to waste it. Here's what you must judge: Do I have a qualified prospect in this person? If so, how good? Rate the prospect A, B, C,

D, E, or F. You must decide if you can spend more time with the prospect if the prospect is any less than an A or perhaps a B. If you have A and B prospects to be working with, you surely wouldn't want to put them off to be working with a C, D, E, or F. One of the best working rules for a salesperson is the old rule "Do things in the order of their importance." That also applies to rating prospects.

YOUR DECISIONS ARE A REFLECTION OF YOUR ABILITY

At this point you must make some major decisions:

1. Is this person a qualified prospect? If not, you will want to abort the interview and move on to greener pastures.
2. Since you have decided the prospect is qualified, you must now decide if you want to move right into the selling presentation or take all of the information with you, prepare a sales presentation, and return at a later date for the actual sales interview.

Regardless of which way you decide to sell, your next step is the selling presentation. If you decide to go ahead with the sales interview right now, you must move very quickly by keeping the prospect's mind open and asking for more. You must now decide exactly how you are going to sell the prospect. You must decide what has to be done to close the sale.

If you are leaving to come back at a later date for the sales talk, be sure you schedule a definite appointment before you leave the prospect.

OBJECTIVE QUESTIONING BUILDS A SALES FOUNDATION THAT WON'T CRUMBLE

OBJECTIVE QUESTIONING AND ACCURATE ANALYSIS WILL GIVE YOU COMPLETE KNOWLEDGE OF THE PROSPECT'S SITUATION. When used early in the interview, it paves the way to an intelligent and successful sales presentation, yet it is a very neglected part of the selling process. The more accurately you determine your prospect's primary interest and dominant buying motive, the more your sales are going to increase.

I urge you to keep the following situations well in mind when building your closing foundation:

1. Prospects don't always buy what they need.
2. Prospects many times buy things they don't need, but want.
3. Prospects only buy what they need or want when sufficient want has been created.

Throughout this book I will give you many ideas to build into your sales presentations to help you to turn the prospect's need and/or want into enough want to make him or her buy.

Champion closers are professional question askers, excellent motivators, and strong want creators. They know exactly what has to be done to get the prospect's business, and that's the secret of closing the sale.

In summary, champion closers build a sale on a good, solid foundation just like contractors erect buildings on solid, firm foundations. If the foundation isn't solid it crumbles, and the entire building crashes and is lost. Sales also are lost and crumble when their foundations aren't solid.

THOUGHT-PROVOKING QUOTES

Hold yourself responsible for a higher standard than anybody else expects of you.
HENRY WARD BEECHER

An opportunity is a favorable occasion for grasping a disappointment.
AMBROSE BIERCE

If you don't do your own thinking, someone else will do it for you.
EDWARD DE BONO

Education is to teach men not what to think but how to think.
CALVIN COOLIDGE

He that fails today may be up again tomorrow.
MIGUEL DE CERVANTES

If your endeavors are beset by fearful odds, and you receive no present reward, go not back to error, nor become a sluggard in the race. When the smoke of battle clears away, you will discern the good you have done and receive according to your deserving.

MARY BAKER EDDY

Don't bother just to be better than your contemporaries or predecessors. Try to be better than yourself.

WILLIAM FAULKNER

Human society is ordered, productive, and in accord with human dignity only if it is based on truth.

POPE JOHN XXIII

Few things are impracticable in themselves, and it is for want of application rather than of means that men fail of success.

LA ROCHEFOUCAULD

All men dream: but not equally. Those who dream at night in the dusty recesses of their minds wake in the day to find that it was vanity: but the dreamers of the day are dangerous men, for they may act their dream with open eyes, to make it possible.

T. E. LAWRENCE

My greatest inspiration is a challenge to attempt the impossible.

ALBERT A. MICHELSON

If a man does not have an ideal, then he becomes a mean, base, and sordid creature, no matter how successful.

THEODORE ROOSEVELT

Little drops of water wear down big stones.

RUSSIAN PROVERB

Defeat should never be a source of discouragement, but rather a fresh stimulus.

ROBERT SOUTH

chapter five

OPEN PROSPECTS' MINDS— MAKE THEM EAGER TO LISTEN

Anyone who stops learning is old, whether this happens at twenty or eighty. Anyone who keeps on learning not only remains young, but also becomes constantly more valuable.
HARVEY ULLMAN

GOOD MIND-OPENING STATEMENTS HELP TO ENSURE SUCCESSFUL CLOSES

"If you have knowledge, let others light their candles from it." Those are the words of Thomas Fuller. To me, that represents what selling is all about. Once a person has product knowledge and motivation there is a logical selling sequence made up of five things to do to satisfy the buyer's mind, which will help to ensure a salesperson's success in closing the sale—to help others light their candles from the benefits of your product and your knowledge.

Whether you get to share your knowledge and the benefits of your product with your prospects depends on how well you can open their minds and make them want to listen to you. You must make the prospect want to listen immediately. Prospects make fast decisions about whether or not they are going to accept you. If you lose the prospect and fail to open the mind properly, the odds are that you have lost the sale. You should place a great amount of thought on your mind-opening statement. Exactly how are you going to kill "I'm not interested," a statement that has shot down many salespeople? Good mind-opening statements are a must if there is going to be a close.

THE LOGICAL WAY TO TELL YOUR STORY

There is a simple track to run, a logical sequence of five things to do to bring about a successful close:

1. Open prospects' minds—make them eager to listen.
2. Keep the mind open and asking for more.
3. Make the prospect feel sure.
4. Develop a sufficient motivating want.
5. Close the sale.

This chapter will cover the period before meeting the prospect and the six ways to open prospects' minds and make them eager to listen. The other four steps will be covered in following chapters.

THE MENTAL-CONDITIONING PERIOD JUST PRIOR TO MEETING THE PROSPECT

The thinking of the salesperson just before meeting the prospect is as tremendously important as the first minute you meet the prospect face to face. Sales are made and lost by the salesperson's thinking prior to the actual meeting with the prospect. Your thoughts during this period will determine the type of first impression you make as well as the outcome of your sales presentation. Favorable first impressions are vital because there is no second chance after making a bad impression.

THE CHALLENGE OF SELLING LIKE A PRO. Let's set the scene. It's appointment time, right day and right hour. You are right on time. On your way to the prospect's location you reaffirm your belief in yourself and your product. You realize that the sale starts right now, in your mind. It's up to you; no one else can sell for you. Success or failure is in your hands. As soon as you park your car, you realize that the prospect may be forming an image of you—the way you walk, your actions. You have done your homework and you are ready for positive action. Now you are making your last-minute mental review about how, from what you now know, you can best serve this prospect. You know exactly how you are going to open this prospect's mind. (If you haven't figured out a mind-opening statement, you will certainly not feel at ease, and rightly so!) You tell yourself again that you can handle this prospect with ease and confidence. In your mind you can see the sale being made successfully. You know every sale is new and different; that is why you love to sell!

You know that you like people and that you will like this prospect very much. You know that the mind-opening step of the selling process is just as important as the close, because if you fail here there won't be a close. You know that many times you won't get a second chance; if the prospect says no and really means it, it is very difficult to get back in again. As you are headed toward the meeting place, you remind yourself you must walk briskly and talk enthusiastically to meet this challenge of selling like a real pro. Say this over at least three times before you actually meet the prospect:

> My prospect deserves the best from me,
> so I'll speak to him or her enthusiastically!

OPEN THE MIND BY EARNING
THE PROSPECT'S INTEREST

WHEN THE PROSPECT TELLS YOU "I'M NOT INTERESTED," HE OR SHE IS TELLING THE TRUTH. Why should the prospect be interested? I am amazed at how many salespeople think they can go into a prospect's office or home for the first time, meet the prospect, and expect to open the prospect's mind by saying, "I'm Henry Brown with the Doe Manufacturing Company." Then the prospect says, "I'm not interested." The prospect is telling the truth. Why should the prospect be interested? What has the salesperson done to earn the prospect's interest and to make him or her eager to listen? The prospect does not care about you and does not care about your company. Prospects are only human. They only care about themselves, their companies, their families, and the various problems they have to solve.

To put it another way, when the prospect sees you, he or she is probably saying to himself or herself, "Why is this person taking up my valuable time?" and "What can this person do for me?" or "Why is this person bothering me?" Since this is on the prospect's mind, why not tell him or her why you are there and what you can do for this prospect right at the very start, before he or she has a chance to say, "I'm not interested."

A favorable impression must be made within a few seconds after you are face to face with the prospect. Many salespeople tell me that the hardest part of the interview is the first minute or so, breaking the ice. Many have told me, "I'm OK after I get started with the prospect, but it's the getting started that's difficult." It's not difficult when you concentrate on your goal of opening the mind with a short mind-opening statement that will kill the words, "I'm not interested." An effective mind-opening statement does not need to be lengthy. In fact, the more brief, clear, and specific it is, the better. One to three well-worded sentences are sufficient. It's *what* you communicate and the *way* you communicate it that are really important.

THE SIX WAYS TO OPEN PROSPECTS' MINDS AND MAKE THEM EAGER TO LISTEN

1. EXCITING IDEAS. Take exciting ideas to your prospect. For example, "Mr. Jones, I've got an exciting idea for you that could possibly help you to reach out and get more customers, increase your repeat customer business, and at the same time cut your advertising budget about 10 percent. I represent the Black and White Company. By the way, my name is Jack Peters."

Another example: "Ms. Smith, I've got some new, exciting ideas for you that I'm sure could save you a lot of time, trouble and unnecessary loss of money in the planning of your estate. By the way, I represent the XWY Company. My name is Tim Jones."

Note that the very first thing I told the prospect was why I was there and what I could do for him or her. Then I quickly added my company and the last thing was my name. It works. Try it. This approach is so simple and easy to use, yet very effective and very neglected.

If you are not comfortable putting your company name and your name at the last part of the statement, put your name first, your company name next, and then immediately bring in your mind-opening statement. But, I repeat, do not expect your name and/or your company name to open the prospect's mind. It won't.

"Good afternoon, Mr. Jones. I'm Jack Peters, representing the Black and White Company. I've got an exciting idea for you that could possibly help you to reach out and get more customers, greatly increase your repeat customer business, and at the same time cut your advertising budget about 10 percent. Does your schedule permit us 30 minutes now to discuss this important matter, or would tomorrow at 9:00 A.M. be better for you?"

"Good morning, Mrs. Smith. I'm Tim Jones, representing the XWY Company. I've got some new, exciting ideas for you that I'm sure could save you a lot of time, trouble, and an unnecessary loss of money in the planning of your estate. Does your schedule permit us 30 minutes right now to discuss this very important matter, or would tomorrow at 2:00 P.M. be more convenient?"

Again, use your name and your company's name where it is most comfortable for you. If you use them at the start, your mind-opening statement must come immediately afterward.

Immediately after your mind-opening statement, if you are not there on a firm appointment, firm up the time (right now or later). If it's firmed now, go ahead with your selling process as outlined. If you are meeting the prospect later on a firm appointment, breaking the ice can be done very easily by simply introducing yourself, using some small talk, repeating your mind-opener, and getting your sales presentation information by asking questions.

These mind-opening statements also can be used on the telephone in making your appointment, or they can be used in writing a letter to the prospect to be followed up by a telephone call. The only change would be advising the prospect that you will call on a certain date and time to set up an appointment.

2. THE REFERRAL. An example: "Mr. Jones, our mutual friend Jack Robbins suggested to me that I should share an idea with you that could possibly save you about 15 percent on your homeowner's policy. That's exactly what I was able to save him. By the way, I represent the Dokes Company. My name is Harry Dokes."

Or: "Mr. Jones, I'm Harry Dokes with the Dokes Company. Our mutual friend Jack Robbins suggested to me that I should share an idea with you that could possibly save you about 15 percent on your homeowner's policy. That's exactly what I was able to save him."

"Ms. Canny, as I mentioned on the phone last evening, Ms. Jackson, an employee of the XCY Company where you work, suggested I share an idea with you. This idea helped her to gain a promotion and a nice pay raise. I'm vice-president of the JJJ Company. My name is Robert Doe."

3. COMPLIMENT. Everyone likes a sincere compliment. It must be sincere and come from the heart—no flattery. "Mr. Smith, con-

gratulations on your great leadership job of turning the YYY Company around and winning the Outstanding Executive Award at the Chamber of Commerce banquet last week. I stopped in to congratulate you and to discuss an exciting idea that could help you to keep the positive momentum going for you with your employees and perhaps help you to win that Outstanding Executive Award again next year. I'm Jim Cass, National Sales Manager for the Greene Company."

"Mr. Doke, your secretary is outstanding. She's a pro at calling people by name, putting them at ease, and making people welcome to your office. She makes a good first impression, Mr. Doke. I congratulate you on the fine training you have given her. Mr. Doke, I'm Bill Able, representing the Overall Company."

4. ASK A QUESTION THAT WILL GET A POSITIVE RESPONSE. "Ms. Gill, everything I read about you in the trade publication magazine indicates that you are the type of sales manager who is constantly searching for effective ideas to help your salespeople do an even better job. That's correct, isn't it? I represent the TTT Company, and my name is Harry Adams." Be sure it's a good, sound basic question, one that will get you a yes response.

"Mr. Hill, Ms. Jackson told me you were the type of leader who is always trying to build your people, keep their morale high, and get even more production from them. Is that correct? By the way, I'm Jack Brooks from the CCC Company."

5. AN EXHIBIT. Anything you can build in the way of an exhibit or demonstration is very worthwhile. Seeing something is worth a thousand words of description. "Ms. Black, I've got an exciting, time-tested, and proven idea for you, one that can save you lots of frustration, time, trouble, and many dollars in needless service calls. [Show exhibit.] You certainly want to keep this situation from happening to you, don't you, Ms. Black? I'm Bob Baker with the Keep 'Em Kleen Company."

"Mr. Harris, I have outlined a minor departmental change for you that could possibly help you save 100 employee hours per month and still increase the production of your people. [Show exhibit.] I represent the KFW Company. I'm Frank Wells."

6. AN EXAMPLE. "Good morning, Mr. Jones. I'm Ted West, representing the CNC Company. We recently did some work for a

well-known company you are probably familiar with, the XYR Company. We were able to save them about $250 per month on their energy bill. We might be able to do the same thing for you. Our estimates are free. Is your schedule open now for about 20 minutes, or would tomorrow at 3:00 P.M. be better for you?"

"Good afternoon, Ms. Lewis. I'm Hal Clark, representing the BBB Company. One of our national accounts, the RVR Company, just informed us by letter of some statistics you might be interested in. In a nutshell, we increased their floor traffic 18 percent, and at the same time cut their advertising expenses 25 percent. As company president, I know you are looking for ways to help your company make even more profit. Is your schedule clear now for about 30 minutes, or would tomorrow at 10:00 A.M. be better?"

A customer list is an excellent place to find many examples. Showing your prospect a customer list while you are relating your example makes this type of mind opener even more effective.

YOU CAN USE VARIOUS COMBINATIONS OF THESE DIFFERENT MIND OPENERS. How you use mind openers depends on your circumstances. Use the one, or any combination of the six, that will make you feel comfortable and will help you to be the most effective. If you have a scheduled appointment, you might introduce yourself, have two or three minutes of small talk, and then give the body of your mind opener. From there get into your questions to gather background information.

NEVER ASSUME THAT THE PROSPECT'S MIND IS OPEN AND RECEPTIVE. Just because a prospect is looking at you doesn't mean you have his or her mind open. The prospect could be thinking about many other things and still be looking right at you. A closed mind will never be receptive and eager to listen to you. It takes very little time to use a mind-opening statement. This technique makes you feel much more relaxed and at ease because you know exactly what you are going to say to the prospect to melt those early icicles.

REGULAR CUSTOMERS MUST HAVE THEIR MINDS REOPENED WHEN YOU PRESENT NEW PRODUCTS, NEW CONCEPTS, AND NEW PROMOTIONS. Just because a customer is buying from you now doesn't mean that customer will be receptive to a new product, new promotion, or new concept. Never assume that the customer's mind is open. You must use an effective mind opener when presenting anything new or different. It's just like calling on a new prospect or opening a new account.

MAKE RECEPTION ROOM TIME PAY DIVIDENDS

The reception room often has valuable information for you to collect. Frequently companies display some of their products, various awards that have been won, copies of the house magazine or weekly bulletins, and sometimes photos of various executives or pictures of their products being used. You can get a good flavor of the atmosphere that exists behind the reception room door by watching the people going in and out and by listening to the way the receptionist handles people and phone calls.

Observe not only the secretary but also other employees who come in and out. Listen and watch them carefully, because an organization is a shadow of the management. These people can give you some valuable clues about your prospect.

Be a good listener and observer. It helps to make waiting time in reception rooms pay dividends.

DON'T UNDERESTIMATE THE POWER
OF THE SECRETARY

YOUR ONE BEST WAY TO GET PAST THE SECRETARY AND SEE YOUR PROSPECT IS BY HAVING A GOOD PERSONALITY. Don't underestimate the power and influence of the secretary. Use your best human relations in a businesslike yet friendly way. Do not fall into the trap of trying to butter up the secretary. That is very poor manners and may cost you the privilege of seeing your prospect. When introducing yourself to the secretary, be courteous, have a pleasant expression on your face, be appreciative, and make sure you get her name correctly. When visiting with her, call her by name. If you have been in the reception room for a few minutes, pay her a sincere compliment and make her feel important just like you would the prospect. Your remarks must come from your heart and be genuine—not flattery.

If the receptionist is extremely busy, don't bother her. She's got her job to do. But if she is not busy, try to carry on a short, general ice-breaking conversation and then ask her a few questions to get some information that would be helpful to you about the prospect. Reception room time doesn't have to be dead time if it is used correctly.

GOOD HUMAN RELATIONS ALWAYS PAY OFF. Several years ago, I was called to Lexington, Kentucky, to be interviewed for a possible one-week consulting job. There were three other very well-qualified candidates being interviewed that day by the board, a group of four men. I was the fourth and last person to be called in. When the secretary called me at my hotel to advise me of a slight change in my appointment time, I made sure to get her name and expressed my sincere appreciation for the phone call. On arrival at the office, I immediately called her by name and used the best human relations principles I could think of. I knew that the other three professionals ahead of me all had excellent credentials. I felt that personality and human relations would go a long way in getting the contract. When the secretary wasn't busy, I addressed her in conversational ice-breaking talk, making sure to call her by name. She gave me some extremely valuable information about what the four board members wanted done, but the payoff came when she said, "You are so good and thoughtful at calling people by name, and you've taken a sincere interest in me and in the board. I am going to give you the names and some background information on the board members that you will be meeting with. This will be very helpful to you." She was right. It was helpful. That thoughtful secretary and the good human relations won me the contract over three very well-qualified competitors.

Never underestimate the power of secretaries. They can be tremendously helpful in getting you in to see the executive behind the door and supplying you with valuable information.

Be sure to stop by the receptionist's or secretary's desk and express your appreciation on the way out.

STRONG MIND OPENERS EQUAL MORE CLOSES

Grace Moore said, "Analyzing what you haven't got as well as what you have is a necessary ingredient of a career." Analyze and build strong mind-opening statements. It will help you to kill the words that haunt so many salespeople: "I'm not interested." Your closing ratio will jump to new highs, and you'll have fun and enjoy making favorable impressions with new prospects.

THOUGHT-PROVOKING QUOTES

If you wish success in your life, make perseverance your bosom friend, experience your wise counsellor, caution your elder brother, and hope your guardian genius.
JOSEPH ADDISON

Our business in life is not to get ahead of other people, but ahead of ourselves.
MALTBIE D. BABCOCK

Destiny is not a matter of chance, it is a matter of choice; it is not a thing to be waited for, it is a thing to be achieved.
WILLIAM JENNINGS BRYAN

Cultivation is as necessary to the mind as food is to the body.
CICERO

Kites rise against, not with, the wind. No man ever worked his passage anywhere in a dead calm.
ROBERT HERRICK

The difference between intelligence and education is this: intelligence will make you a good living.
CHARLES F. KETTERING

New opinions are always suspected and usually opposed, for no other reason than because they are not already common.
JOHN LOCKE

There is only one success—to be able to spend your life in your own way.
CHRISTOPHER MORLEY

The size of a man can be measured by the size of the thing that makes him angry.
J. KENFIELD MORLEY

A large part of virtue consists in good habits.
WILLIAM PALEY

At a certain age some people's minds close up; they live on their intellectual fat.

WILLIAM LYON PHELPS

If you have made mistakes, even serious ones, there is always another chance for you. What we call failure is not the falling down, but the staying down.

MARY PICKFORD

The mind itself must, like other things, sometimes be unbent; or else it will be either weakened or broken.

PHILIP SIDNEY

The only sense that is common in the long run, is the sense of change . . . and we all instinctively avoid it.

E. B. WHITE

chapter six

KEEP THE MIND
OPEN AND ASKING
FOR MORE

Either I will find a way or I will make one.
PHILIP SIDNEY

THE ACTUAL PRESENTATION STARTS HERE

YOU (OR YOUR COMPANY) HAVE AN INVESTMENT OF TIME AND MONEY IN EVERY PROSPECT. Your job is to get that investment back and perhaps a whole lot more. There have been transportation expenses, phone calls, advertising expenses, out-of-pocket prospecting expenses, some time involved. To stay in the selling profession you must produce. Nothing counts (half-sales don't count) unless the sale is closed!

THE THREE CRITICAL FACTORS YOU MUST KNOW
AT THIS STAGE

FIRST, YOU MUST BE ABLE TO TELL, FULLY AND SPECIFICALLY, THE WHOLE PRODUCT STORY. It must be well-organized and made for this specific prospect. You must have complete product knowledge, be confident, and be able to answer any questions the prospect may ask about what it is, how it is made, what it will do, and what it will mean in terms of related benefits to your prospect.

SECOND, YOU MUST BE SATISFIED THAT YOU HAVE COMPLETE BACKGROUND KNOWLEDGE OF THE PROSPECT. You must be sure that you know the need and/or want and the prospect's exact motive or, putting it another way, the prospect's primary interest (PI) and the dominant buying motive (DBM). You must be able to tailor your product benefits creatively to fulfill that PI and DBM.

THIRD, YOU MUST HAVE ARMED YOURSELF AND HAVE CLEARLY IN MIND HOW YOU ARE GOING TO USE YOUR SELLING SKILLS IN ORDER TO CLOSE THE SALE SUCCESSFULLY. For example, it starts right here: How are you going to keep the mind open and asking for more? Also, you must know the answer to every stall or objection that might come up. You should know the objections that your competitors get and be able to capitalize on those. In front of the prospect is no place to stammer and stutter while making a sales presentation.

Your various selling skills and product knowledge should be memorized. But do not memorize every word of your sales talk from A to Z, from start to finish. Completely canned presentations usually come out artificially, with very little flexibility, originality, and empathy used. The odds are that a completely canned presentation will not make the sale by itself. It's the ability and personality of the salesperson that closes the sale. The ability to be flexible, to tailor and bend the important memorized sales tract parts and materials to solve the prospect's problem wins the signed order. The salesperson's ability to use empathy, to periodically use trial closes, and to watch and listen for closing signals enables the salesperson to ask for the order at the right time. That salesperson keeps things moving in a positive direction right to the close!

THINK AND REMAIN COOL UNDER PRESSURE

BE READY—HAVE INSTANT RECALL POWER FROM YOUR KNOWLEDGE BANK. Six words by Eddie Rickenbacker sum up success: "Think things through—then follow through." Study and have at the tip of your tongue everything mentioned in the three critical factor areas. As I said in chapter 4, creative selling involves making an accurate mental sales outline. Keep this outline and all of the important points well in mind. Think before you speak. Nothing gives one person so much advantage over another as to always remain cool and unruffled under all circumstances.

Andrew Carnegie said, "I believe the true road to preeminent success in any line is to make yourself master of that line." Here's where your professionalism will really pay off. While being your best and being the master of all situations, you will be staying in charge and keeping the presentation moving and flowing smoothly. You will be able to analyze and know where you are at all times. You will quickly sense what has to be done at the right time. You'll dip into your instant recall knowledge bank and, without any hesitation or excessively long pauses, bring into the presentation everything necessary for a successful close. Nothing will be left out.

It is very upsetting for me to watch salespeople who have spent many dollars and much time get in front of qualified prospects and then strike out by making an incomplete and inadequate sales presentation. All of that time and money was wasted! When an interview has been messed up, I know of no easy reentry method that will get that salesperson back in the door. The prospect will remember that sour sorrowful experience for a long time. A bad impression was made by the salesperson and, unfortunately, the company. It could take a long time and a great amount of work to have the opportunity of making a sales presentation to that prospect again.

TO CLOSE LATER, GIVE YOUR PROSPECT
REASSURANCE NOW

YOU MUST BUILD ON THIS SALE'S FOUNDATION WITHOUT HESITATION. You opened the prospect's mind and you have successfully obtained and/or verified all necessary selling information about the prospect. The sale's foundation is strong and will hold up the rest of the selling process. You have decided that you have a qualified prospect. Now, still on the first call, you can continue on with your sales presentation with reassurance.

If this is the start of the second call (you opened the mind, got important information on first call, and left to prepare your sales talk) immediately give reassurance and then go on into your sales talk. At the end of the short reassurance step, you want your prospect saying, "Tell me more. This sounds great. How is this going to be done?"

"MR. PROSPECT, FROM WHAT YOU HAVE TOLD ME, I CAN ASSURE YOU THAT . . ." To keep the mind open and asking for more is really quite simple. In fact, it's so simple that it is overlooked by many salespeople. Yet it is vitally important. The prospect wants and needs reassurance at this point. This reassurance step should be brief, clear, and specific. Two or three well-thought-out sentences are plenty. Your key words are, "Mr. Prospect, from what you have told me, I can assure you that . . ." That phrase is very helpful in keeping the mind open and asking for more.

For example, "Ms. Doe, from what you have told me, I can assure you that our model XY machine will give you exactly what you want in this type of machine. It will save you about 100 employee hours every week, reduce complaints, and help you to get the payroll out on time, thus increasing your chances for a promotion because your department will save about $5,000 a month in labor alone."

In your reassurance step, make a claim or promise about exactly what you or your product can do. Continue talking strictly in the prospect's interest. I know buyers don't buy claims and promises, but remember your goal here is to keep the mind open and asking for more. You must be prepared to back up and prove your claim or promise, which is the next logical step of the selling process.

YES RESPONSES STRENGTHEN YOUR POSITION

Another method of keeping the mind open and asking for more is to restate the primary interest and the dominant buying motive and get a *yes* response. "Mr. Smith, I want to make sure I understand everything correctly. From what you told me, I am of the opinion that you want a five-bedroom house, new or in first-class condition, with ample room for entertaining your associates. You want something that will create the executive-type image, thus improving your chances for a promotion and bringing home a larger paycheck. Is this correct?"

Now the reassurance: "Mr. Smith, from what you have told me, I can assure you that I have three prestigious five-bedroom homes in my listings, all of which are what you want—lots of room for first-class entertaining and designed to help you create a favorable executive image, thus enhancing, from what you have said, your chances for a promotion and a bigger paycheck."

The prospect's mind is now open and asking for more. The primary interest (what the prospect needs and/or wants) in this case is a five-bedroom house. The dominant buying motive (why it is wanted, the end result) is a promotion, profit, a bigger paycheck. Every time you get a yes response, you are closer to total agreement.

NEVER ASSUME THE PROSPECT'S MIND IS STILL OPEN AND ASKING FOR MORE

It is dangerous to assume that the prospect's mind is still open. Why take the chance of talking to a closed mind and have the interview terminated, when it is so simple and easy to keep the sales interview headed right for the successful close?

The prospect is now saying to himself or herself, "I want more information. How is this salesperson going to do this for me? The salesperson will have to prove to me that it can be done." That's exactly what you want your prospect thinking.

Now, on to the next step—making the prospect feel sure.

THOUGHT-PROVOKING QUOTES

I find that a great deal of the information I have was acquired by looking up something and finding something else on the way.
FRANKLIN P. ADAMS

By taking revenge, a man is but even with his enemy; but in passing over it, he is superior.
FRANCIS BACON

Education makes people easy to lead, but difficult to drive, easy to govern, but impossible to enslave.
HENRY BROUGHAM

A man in earnest finds means, or if he cannot find, creates them.
WILLIAM ELLERY CHANNING

One should . . . be able to see things as hopeless and yet be determined to make them otherwise.
F. SCOTT FITZGERALD

There is trouble and sorrow enough in the world, without making it on purpose.
WILLIAM DEAN HOWELLS

A failure is a man who blundered, but is not able to cash in on the experience.
ELBERT HUBBARD

The course of every intellectual, if he pursues his journey long and unflinchingly enough, ends in the obvious, from which the nonintellectuals have never stirred.
ALDOUS HUXLEY

Thinking is one thing no one has ever been able to tax.
CHARLES F. KETTERING

The highest achievement of man is a program for discontent.
HERMANN JOSEPH MULLER

Men in condition do not tire. High physical condition is vital to victory.
GEORGE S. PATTON JR.

We need to teach our children that they can't cheat. There is no way to pull it off: You can't lie to life. You may deceive your teacher about what you know, but you can't deceive life. What you haven't learned leaves a hole that nothing but that learning can fill and no amount of covering over can disguise.
EDWARD R. SIMS

I know of no more encouraging fact than the unquestionable ability of man to elevate his life by a conscious endeavor.
HENRY DAVID THOREAU

A little learning is not a dangerous thing to one who does not mistake it for a great deal.
WILLIAM ALLEN WHITE

chapter seven

MAKE THE PROSPECT FEEL SURE

It is not a question how much a man knows, but what
use he makes of what he knows. Not a question of
what he has acquired and how he has been trained,
but of what he is and what he can do.
J. G. HOLLAND

PROSPECTS DO NOT BUY UNTIL ALL DOUBTS
AND FEARS HAVE VANISHED

A CLAIM OR PROMISE KEEPS THE MIND OPEN AND ASKING FOR MORE
ABOUT YOUR PRODUCT. The claim or promise served its purpose. It
got you to this next logical step in selling the prospect. Now your
challenge is to make the prospect feel sure that your claim or promise is true. Buyers do not buy claims and promises. You know what
you have claimed or promised is true, but your prospect doesn't. It's
only natural that the prospect has doubt and fear at this point in the
sales interview. You have done nothing so far to convince the
prospect. Webster defines the word *convince* as "to overcome the
doubts of; to persuade by argument or evidence; make feel sure."
The prospect will never buy until he or she feels justified, until you
have made him or her feel sure and all doubts and fears have been
removed.

THE THREE BASIC FEARS OF A PROSPECT

BASIC FEAR 1. ONE OF THE FIRST THINGS A PROSPECT BECOMES FEARFUL
OF IS YOU. YOU ARE A SALESPERSON AND HE OR SHE DOESN'T KNOW YOU.
The prospect probably has heard rumors of friends being "taken to
the cleaners" by a salesperson; people who put money down, didn't
go ahead with the purchase, and couldn't get their money back. The
prospect has been told by a friend, "Never buy anything from a
salesperson you don't know." The prospect has heard many things,
some true and some not true. It's a condition you have to handle.
Prospects feel that you might be there to cheat them, that they might
lose money, or that they will not receive their money's worth. The
prospect may feel that it might be better to cancel the whole idea of
buying from you and hang on to his or her money. As a result, the
prospect may tell you that he or she can't afford your product. The
prospect is simply afraid to part with the money. Everyone is fearful
of losing money.

BASIC FEAR 2. THE PROSPECT IS AFRAID THAT THE PRODUCT MAY NOT BE OF THE HIGH QUALITY YOU SAID IT WAS. The product might be faulty, second-rate, inferior, or won't do what the prospect needs or wants done. The prospect has doubts because he or she isn't a qualified expert in all types of merchandise, products, and services. When the prospect is buying something for the first time, he or she feels uneasy and unsure, and fear grabs hold.

BASIC FEAR 3. THE PROSPECT CAN HAVE A GREAT AMOUNT OF FEAR OVER WHAT OTHER PEOPLE WILL THINK OF THE DECISION TO BUY FROM YOU. The prospect is afraid of what the board of directors might think, what his or her spouse might think, what the neighbors will say. The prospect doesn't want to make an unwise decision to buy for fear of being laughed at, for fear the decision to buy will backfire and will reflect his or her poor judgment, for fear of criticism.

To make the prospect feel completely justified in his or her mind and to overcome these three basic fears, here are four points that must be proven in the buyer's mind. Then and only then will the prospect feel sure.

1. You must prove that it is a good product or service.
2. You must prove that it will do what the prospect needs and/or wants done, that it will fulfill the primary interest and the dominant buying motive.
3. You must prove that it is worth the asking price.
4. You must prove that the prospect is justified in deciding to buy right now.

PROOF MUST BE TAILORED FOR EACH PROSPECT

BY PROVING THESE FOUR POINTS, YOU HAVE AUTOMATICALLY OVERCOME THE THREE BASIC FEARS. I caution you to be flexible and tailor your proof. What will serve as proof to one individual may not be proof to another individual. It's very important to have proof for all types of prospects using the proper proof to satisfy and overcome each individual's particular fears.

IF YOU CAN PROVE A CLAIM OR PROMISE, AND YOU'D BETTER BE ABLE TO, THEN YOU HAVE KEPT THE PROSPECT'S MIND OPEN, AND THE CLAIM OR PROMISE BECOMES A FACT. Webster defines *proof* as "the act of proving; the establishment of the truth of something; to convince one of the truth; conclusive evidence." A claim or promise becomes a fact in the buyer's mind when it is completely accepted without any doubt or question. But keep in mind that buyers do *not* buy claims, promises, or even facts. Buyers only buy related buyer's benefits. I have stressed this many times throughout this book.

"Magnificent promises are always to be suspected," said Theodore Parker. How many times have you heard someone, after he or she has just left a salesperson, say, "Well, according to the salesperson, this will do so and so. That's what he claimed. I don't believe him, but that's what he claimed"? Obviously, the salesperson didn't make the sale. Unproven claims and promises rarely close the sale. The buyer did not get the proof necessary for him or her to accept the claim without doubt and question. Proof, facts, and related buyer's benefits were never given.

Perhaps you have heard an automobile salesperson say, "This car is absolutely the finest car on the market today." You say to yourself, "I'd like to believe you, but I don't. Prove it." Maybe you have heard an insurance salesperson say, "Our company is the safest insurance company in America," or a real estate salesperson say, "Buy this home today and it will be worth twice as much in five years," or an appliance salesperson say, "This refrigerator will last twice as long as the one you just looked at." Those are claims. You must be in a position to prove every claim or promise you make. Mohandas Gandhi said it so well: "Above all, keep yourselves pure and clean, and learn to keep your promises, even at the cost of life."

CONCLUSIVE STRONG EVIDENCE EQUALS MORE CLOSES

There are several very effective forms of strong evidence to help you overcome the buyer's fears and to help you to prove your claims and promises. I encourage you to study these and, from this point on, never make a call without taking some type of strong, convincing evidence with you to help you make the prospect feel sure and to remove all doubts. According to Webster, *evidence* is "something that tends to prove; ground for belief."

TESTIMONIALS. One of the oldest and best forms of proof is testimonials. Get testimonial letters from your customers. Build yourself a neat testimonial book. This is a powerful tool. "Here, Mr. Prospect, are some of the people who have invested in this opportunity, and this is what they have said. Pick up the phone and call any of them, if you wish." Very few salespeople use testimonials in their selling interviews. In many groups, I find only four or five salespeople out of a hundred using testimonials.

Webster defines *testimonial* as "a statement testifying to the merits of some product or service; letter or statement of recommendation."

Handwritten testimonials are just as effective as typewritten ones. The content of the letter is vital, as is the name of the individual or company. Get testimonials from all different types of customers, use the ones that a particular prospect can identify with, and use names that the prospect will respect.

Always ask for permission to use the testimonials from the writer. I recommend getting a signed release.

DEMONSTRATIONS AND SHOWMANSHIP. "I am satisfied that we are less convinced by what we hear than by what we see," said Herodotus. Use sparkling showmanship and make the most striking demonstrations you can to help the prospect see the benefits of your product and to prove your claims and promises. Many times you can get your prospect involved in the act. Everyone likes action and likes to see something that is happening right before his or her eyes. People love good showmanship. They'll enjoy it, and it will prove and sell.

Demonstrations make the claims and/or promises you make very believable. Prospects can see first-hand. Demonstrations and showmanship will liven up your presentation. According to Webster, *showmanship* is "presenting anything in an interesting or dramatic manner." Practice every move. Look professional. It is very difficult to ignore or turn away from an active, well-presented demonstration. Be ready to demonstrate every important point of your product that you possibly can. Demonstrations and showmanship not only help you to keep the prospect's mind open, but they also make your sales presentation interesting, vivid, and much more convincing. Seeing something one time is worth a thousand words of description.

CONCLUSIONS OF STUDIES OR EXPERTS. Be sure to state your source. Exactly what does the source say? Exactly what do the conclusions prove? Are the conclusions current? Make sure your conclusions are compiled by some solid, respectable, reputable source. Conclusions, numbers, findings, and figures certainly help to prove a point. Make sure you present them with color and animation.

SENSUOUS FULFILLMENT. This type of proof is very effective if your product is of a certain type. Here you make the prospect feel sure by letting them taste the product, smell the product, feel the product, see the product, and/or hear the product. What better conclusive personal evidence can you supply? Many times you can be very effective in proving your claim and/or promise by using just one of the senses. If your product is the right kind, you can use a combination of two or more senses.

EXHIBIT. Build a unique and well-organized exhibit. Make sure that your exhibit proves an important point. Pictures, graphs, magazines, scaled-down models, newspaper articles, displays of the actual product, books, charts, blueprints—all of these things can be exhibited and can be quite helpful because it's something that the prospect can see. Things that we see become believable and acceptable.

STORIES MADE UP OF EXAMPLES AND ILLUSTRATIONS. "Example is the school of mankind; they will learn at no other," said Edmund Burke. This is a very powerful and convincing technique. Upon hearing an actual, true story, it is only natural for your prospect to identify with an example of some other person who had and solved a similar problem. When told well, stories containing an example of a person who bought and benefited from your product are most convincing.

Make sure your story proves the point that you want proven. It must be relevant to the selling situation you are now in. Use stories, examples, and names of people your prospect will respect. Invite your prospect to call the person you told about in your story.

Stories of satisfied customers should be plentiful. Take the time and really work at polishing your stories. Have one or two stories at the tip of your tongue to prove every important point you want to bring out. Be sure each story is complete and that you have answered *who, what, where, how, when,* and *why.* Any story that is not complete misses the point. It drags and is boring. It is not going to help you at all. Your stories must capture and hold the attention of your busy prospect, just like a speaker must capture and hold the attention of an audience. That means you must rehearse and practice telling your stories until perfection is achieved. I believe telling stories properly is important enough that it warrants a salesperson spending hours of preparation time.

CUSTOMER LIST. This is a powerful confidence builder to make the prospect feel sure. It is one of the most effective tools a salesperson has. The prospect wants to feel comfortable and the minute he or she sees the names and addresses of prominent customers who have purchased your product a strong reassurance develops.

It's an easy tool for you to obtain. Just write up a complete list of your most prominent customers with addresses. It's helpful to make your list as diversified as possible so that your prospect can relate to his or her own kind of business.

GUARANTEE. Show a copy of your guarantee and make a brief explanation of it. Explain the conditions and the length of time the product is guaranteed for. A strong guarantee makes an excellent convincing tool.

A PROVEN CLAIM OR PROMISE BECOMES A FACT

Webster defines *fact* as "a thing that has actually happened or that is really true; the state of things as they really are; reality, actuality; truth." When you prove a claim or promise, it becomes factual, a reality, a truth. "This boat has a 170-horsepower engine." "This lamp comes with an 18-foot cord." "This recreation room is 12 feet by 24 feet." These are facts.

TURN FACTS INTO RELATED BUYER'S BENEFITS

When you state a fact to the prospect, you still have not told the prospect what this fact means to him or her. To make your facts meaningful and really sell the prospect, state your fact, follow that with a personalized bridge, and then state a related buyer's benefit. According to Webster, to *bridge* is "to provide a connection, transition." The bridge serves as the connector. It connects the fact to the related buyer's benefit. Personalize the connector or bridge by always using *you* and/or sometimes the prospect's name.

FACT → PERSONALIZED BRIDGE → RELATED BUYER'S BENEFIT

An example: "The recreation room in this house is 12 feet by 24 feet (fact), which is important to you, Ms. Smith (personalized bridge) because this will give you adequate room for entertaining (related buyer's benefit)."

Make it a firm rule that every time you state a fact about your product you will follow it with a personalized bridge; "which is important to you, Ms. Smith," or "which means to you," and then follow that with a related buyer's benefit.

You may use one fact—personalized bridge—related buyer's benefit to help convince the prospect, or you may use two, three, or four facts—personalized bridges—related buyer's benefits to substantiate your claim, following that with evidence and a *yes* response trial close question to get agreement.

BE READY TO CLOSE

DON'T MISS AN OPPORTUNITY TO CLOSE. On getting positive agreement from your *yes* response trial close question, don't overlook a chance to successfully close the sale even though it's early in the interview and you have a great amount of sales material that you haven't used. Every time you get a *yes* response from the prospect you are in a stronger position. The *yes* response question, as used here, is a trial close (see Chapter 9). You can now do one of two things: either use another trial close to get further agreement on some other feature, or if the prospect is really hot, skip another trial close and go directly to the close (Chapter 10).

The following diagram will review what I have said about claims and promises, facts, personalized bridges, related buyer's benefits, evidence, the *yes* response trial close question, and the close.

CLAIM–PROMISE → because → FACT → PERSONALIZED BRIDGE˙→ RELATED BUYER'S BENEFIT˙→ EVIDENCE˙→ *YES* RESPONSE TRIAL CLOSE QUESTION˙→ CLOSE

"This boat is just the right size and has just the right-sized engine to provide your family of eight with the finest in water recreation (claim) because it is powered with a 170-horsepower motor (fact). This is very important to you, Mr. Smith (personalized bridge) as you can have six people in your boat and pull two skiers at the same time (related buyer's benefit). Here are the specifications that have been made up by the XYZ Independent Testing Bureau, a government-approved authority on boat specifications (evidence). It clearly shows that this boat is capable of carrying eight adults or six adults aboard while two people are skiing, exactly what you want in a boat. You do want a boat that will easily handle six adults in the boat and pull two skiers at the same time, don't you? (*yes* response trial close question)." Be alert for an opportunity to close at this point.

Again, depending on the situation you may use two or three facts–personalized bridges–related buyer's benefits in convincing your prospect, in which case the diagram would look like this:

CLAIM–PROMISE
↓
because → FACT → PERSONALIZED BRIDGE →
RELATED BUYER'S BENEFIT

because → FACT → PERSONALIZED BRIDGE →
        RELATED BUYER'S BENEFIT
because → FACT → PERSONALIZED BRIDGE →
        RELATED BUYER'S BENEFIT

EVIDENCE → *YES* RESPONSE TRIAL CLOSE QUESTION → CLOSE

The important thing is that every claim or promise must be proven. The above diagrams show every step necessary for you to be very convincing and to make the prospect feel sure.

DON'T LET THE PROSPECT DO YOUR WORK

Some salespeople today believe that buyers buy claims, promises, and facts. They do not. Perhaps it's because they don't fully understand the difference between a claim–promise, a fact, and a buyer's benefit. Never try to close the sale by shooting wild, exaggerated claim after claim or promise after promise at the prospect. It won't work.

Sometimes salespeople give facts about their product and honestly think that they are actually giving buyer's benefits. There is a big difference. Giving facts about your product and not following it up with a personalized bridge and the related buyer's benefit is like leaving the frosting off the cake; it lacks the best part.

Make a complete list of claims and promises that you use in your interviews, as well as a complete list of every fact and buyer's benefit you might use in an interview. This will help to clear up any misunderstanding.

In a selling interview, never let the prospect supply the benefits to any fact that you state. That's letting the prospect do your work, and he or she will not do it as effectively as you do. It's a mighty dangerous thing to do. Prospects automatically put up sales resistance. People naturally want to build a defense. Many times, because of the three basic buyer's fears, they think up a negative aspect. After hearing three or four facts and then coming up, in their own mind, with three or four negative aspects, they've got a pretty good case built up against the product and/or salesperson. The salesperson has not only made his or her work much more difficult, but he or she also will probably fail to close the sale successfully.

KEY TECHNIQUES TO HELP YOU MAKE THE PROSPECT FEEL SURE

Here are some additional points to consider to convince your prospect and to make your prospect feel sure:

1. NEVER EXAGGERATE. You always weaken whatever you exaggerate. Tryon Edwards spoke the truth when he said, "Some so speak in exaggerations and superlatives that we need to make a large discount from their statements before we can come at their real meaning."

   I put a salesperson who exaggerates in the same category as a salesperson who lies. If you can't sell your product truthfully, then you shouldn't be selling it. Unfortunately, I know of salespeople who exaggerate and the reason they do, in my opinion, is that they don't want to spend the time and energy to do the work necessary to be able to sell all different types of prospects in a legitimate, creative way. They shoot one exaggeration after another at the prospect and then can't figure out why they didn't make the sale.

2. KEEP IT SIMPLE. Use easy, conversational language that everyone can understand. If you must use terms that are unfamiliar to the prospect, follow them immediately with an explanation that will be understood. When a prospect doesn't understand something, interest disappears very rapidly. Don't try to show off or be impressive by using a vocabulary that people do not understand.

3. BE BRIEF. Don't bore the prospect with lots of dull, nonapplicable, nonrelated information. Every call is a selling call and should be handled in a very professional manner. A few well-thought-out rifle shots of conviction will do far more good than many shotgun blasts of misguided, inappropriate, meaningless sales-talk material. Remember, give your prospect just enough conviction to make him or her feel sure about buying your product or service.

4. IF NECESSARY, REPEAT AN IMPORTANT RELATED FACT AND BENEFIT AND GET ANOTHER *YES* RESPONSE FROM A TRIAL CLOSE. It's helpful many times to repeat a key fact–personalized bridge–related buyer's benefit and then immediately ask a *yes* response trial close question. If necessary, show the proof or evidence one more time. This is reassurance and will help the prospect feel more at ease and more sure.

   Keeping the prospect agreeing and paving the way to the close with another *yes* response trial close question is very important and really quite easy. Keeping the prospect's primary interest and dominant buying motive in mind, repeat a fact–personalized bridge–related buyer's benefit and get a *yes* response. For example: "This boat is powered with a 170-horsepower inboard/outboard engine. This is important to you because you can carry six adults in the boat and pull two skiers at the same time. From what you have told me, Mr. Doe, you and your family love boating get-togethers and water skiing, and you want a boat that will comfortably carry six adults and will pull two skiers at the same time. That's correct, isn't it?" A *yes* response trial close comes from merely turning the buyer's benefit into a well-worded question, keeping the primary interest and dominant buying motive well in mind.

5. BE SPECIFIC AND ACCURATE. Zero in on your target. If necessary, continue asking a few questions to confirm and to make sure that you are on track and that you correctly analyzed and know what the target is, the area in which your conviction must be directed.

6. FREQUENTLY ASK, "HAVE I MADE MYSELF CLEAR?" Never ask prospects if they understood what you have said. Prospects hate to admit that they did not understand something for fear they are admitting they are not sharp or not as smart as you are. Instead, say something like this: "Have I made myself clear? I get so excited and involved in this, and there's so much ground to cover, sometimes I fail to make myself clear."

7. NEVER USE THE PHRASE, "I'LL PROVE TO YOU." This point is worth repeating. The minute you tell a prospect that you are going to prove something, you are saying that you are superior. You are putting the prospect down. Instead, say something like this: "In

a minute I'm going to make a demonstration. You'll enjoy it and you will be able to judge for yourself," or "Mr. Doe bought this product and was very concerned about the same point that you are concerned about. After using this product for six months, here's what Mr. Doe says . . . You are invited to call him and talk to him if you would like."

8. NEVER ARGUE. You are with the prospect to make a sale, not to win an ego trip of your own. At times you must disagree with your prospect. That's only natural. Disagreement does not have to turn into an argument. Tactfully, with good human engineering principles, turn the prospect around to your way of thinking. Always keep your self-respect and professional image.

9. STAY CALM, AND NEVER LOSE YOUR TEMPER. The prospect will do things and say things that irritate you. There will be unannounced interruptions. Sometimes the prospect will try to cut the interview short, ask irrelevant questions, or answer the phone. The prospect may even ask you to continue your sales talk while he or she looks over a memo. In short, many things can happen in an interview to make you upset and angry. Do not continue giving your talk until conditions can be made right and you can secure the prospect's attention. Many times, it is better for the salesperson to reschedule the appointment. Be polite; stay calm and collected. Never lose your temper. Think things through and get things back on track as quickly and smoothly as possible. The prospect will admire the way you handle an irritating situation.

10. SPEAK CLEARLY, USING GOOD GRAMMAR. Speak in a pleasant tone, loudly enough to be heard, clearly enough always to be understood, and use good grammar. Bad grammar is very offensive and annoys a lot of people.

AVOID OVERSELL OR OVERKILL

IT'S POSSIBLE FOR YOU TO MAKE THE SALE AND THEN BUY THE PRODUCT BACK! Many times I am asked, "How many facts and benefits do you give in a sales interview?" The cardinal rule is just enough to ensure the close of the sale. Do not oversell! There's only one time to close the sale, and that is when the prospect is ready to buy. It might come early in the interview; it might come late in the interview. You'll be able to tell by effectively using trial closes and closing signals. These are covered in chapter 9.

MANY SALES CAN BE CLOSED RIGHT NOW—SOME REQUIRE MORE PERSUASION

Your goal at this point is to have the prospect feel sure and completely convinced that you do have a good product; that it is worth the asking price; that it will fulfill the prospect's need, want, and motive; and that the prospect is justified in going ahead with it now. The prospect's three basic fears will have been overcome. Many times sales can be closed right at this point in the selling process. Then again, it may take a little more persuasion to make the prospect sufficiently want what he or she really needs or has some degree of want for. This takes us to the next chapter, the fourth step in the selling process, developing a sufficient motivating want.

THOUGHT-PROVOKING QUOTES

Straight is the gate and narrow is the way that leads to reputation, honor, success, and happiness.
JOHN ADAMS

Never render men such service as compels them to be ungrateful, for then they become your implacable enemies.
HONORÉ DE BALZAC

A man's life is interesting primarily when he has failed—I well know. For it's a sign that he tried to surpass himself.
GEORGES CLEMENCEAU

Common sense is genius dressed in its working clothes.
RALPH WALDO EMERSON

Practice yourself in little things, and then proceed to greater.
EPICTETUS

All things are difficult before they are easy.
THOMAS FULLER

Behind many acts that are thought ridiculous there lie wise and weighty motives.
LA ROCHEFOUCAULD

The talent of success is nothing more than doing what you can do well.

> HENRY WADSWORTH
> LONGFELLOW

The successful people are the ones who can think up things for the rest of the world to keep busy at.

> DON MARQUIS

We think too small. Like the frog at the bottom of the well. He thinks the sky is only as big as the top of the well. If he surfaced, he would have an entirely different view.

> MAO TSE-TUNG

What great thing would you attempt if you knew you could not fail?

> ROBERT SCHULLER

We should treat our minds as innocent and ingenuous children whose guardian we are—be careful what objects and what subjects we thrust on their attention.

> HENRY DAVID THOREAU

The most precious thing a parent can give a child is a lifetime of happy memories.

> FRANK TYGER

The only man who can't change his mind is a man who hasn't got one.

> EDWARD NOYES WESCOTT

chapter eight

DEVELOP A SUFFICIENT MOTIVATING WANT

The old mousetrap story was true a hundred years ago and is true today. If we make the best one, and it is priced right, and we serve a thousand people, we prosper. If we serve a million and do it better than our mousetrap competitors, we prosper a thousand-fold, and not because we are capitalistic. We prosper only because we serve more people better than others; we satisfy their wants; we help them along the way.
HUGHSTON MCBAIN

YOU MUST PROVIDE THE RIGHT BALANCE OF
EMOTIONAL APPEAL AND LOGIC

SOME BUYERS REQUIRE MORE EMOTIONAL APPEAL; OTHERS MORE LOGIC. Thus far in your sales presentation, you have been very logical. You have been appealing mainly to the prospect's logic. Professional selling is the proper balance of logic and emotion as determined by each specific selling situation. True, you have been enthusiastic in your sales talk, which is emotion, but for the most part you have concentrated on how to open the prospect's mind logically and keep it open, and you have used logical, strong facts, benefits, and evidence to make the prospect feel sure.

Many sales, as brought out earlier, can be closed immediately after you have made the prospect feel sure. After using your proving evidence, I suggested that you use a trial close, and then that you go right to the close if a positive response is received. In addition, you should always watch and listen for closing signals, and if you receive a strong, positive closing signal, you go right to the close and ask for the order.

Some salespeople, however, like to use a trial close right after a positive closing signal has been received, get a positive response, and then go immediately to the close and ask for the order. That's fine.

The prospect who can be closed earlier in the interview created sufficient want within himself or herself and mentally formed a picture in his or her mind of himself or herself successfully using the end result benefits of your product.

However, let us say you have used a trial close and have watched and listened for closing signals without any positive actions or reactions (see chapter 9). Is there anything else you can do to get the prospect ready for closing? You can develop more emotional appeal and create more want for your product to balance out with the logic you have already given the prospect.

PROSPECTS DON'T ALWAYS BUY JUST BECAUSE YOU HAVE THE BEST PRODUCT

PRODUCTS DON'T SELL THEMSELVES. Many sales are lost each day because the salesperson feels that prospects buy because "it's the best product made." Other salespeople say their product is so good it sells itself. People do not always buy just because you have the best product. You know of many "best" products on the market today that you do not own. You also know many products that are supposed to be so great that they will sell themselves, yet you have not bought them. People buy only when they have a sufficiently strong desire to own a product so that they can get the use and end result benefits. The reason you don't own the best product made and the one that is so good it sells itself is that you do not have a real desire to own that product regardless of how terrific it really is. Even if some people need that best product, they don't always buy it. A *champion closer* is one who can generate *sufficient want* for his or her product, *which motivates* the prospect to buy.

In review of what I said earlier about needs and wants, please consider these very important points and keep them clearly in your mind:

1. Prospects don't always buy what they need.
2. Prospects many times buy things they don't need, but want.
3. *Prospects only buy what they need or want when sufficient want has been created.*

YOU MUST BE A WANT CREATOR

Webster defines create as "to cause to come into existence; bring into being; make; originate." To successfully develop sufficient want in the prospect who cannot be closed earlier in the interview, *you must make him or her mentally see himself or herself successfully using the end result benefits of your product.* Obviously, the prospect hasn't been able to do this without your help or the sale would have been closed earlier.

USE YOUR CREATIVE POWER

Stop and think. Every time you purchased an automobile, re-frigerator, home, boat, washing machine, clothes dryer, or insur-ance policy, you had a positive, vivid mind picture of yourself successfully using the end result benefits of that product. As you think of these various products, think about the motive you had when you made the purchase. Your motive was part of your mind picture. Reviewing these mind pictures will help you to build mind pictures for your prospect.

Use your imagination and creative thinking to project the prospect into an emotional mental picture using your product suc-cessfully. Webster defines *imagination* as "the act or power of form-ing mental images of what is not actually present; the act or power of creating mental images of what has never been actually experienced; creative power; creation of the mind."

EMOTIONAL MENTAL PICTURES WILL CREATE SUFFICIENT STRONG DESIRE FOR YOUR PRODUCT

There are five basic things to do in creating a dynamic mind picture.

1. Restate and verify the prospect's primary interest and dom-inant buying motive. Get his or her agreement. "Mr. Pros-pect, I understand you need and/or want this (PI) because (state why—DBM). Is this correct?" You cannot afford to be wrong. Your emotional appeal must center on this critical information.

2. Give the prospect reassurance. This should be a claim or promise that relates to the points you will use in your mind picture. "Mrs. Smith, from what you have told me, I can assure you that my product will do exactly what you want done."

3. Prove these claims or promises with evidence. *Be very brief.* The emphasis is on emotion, not logic.

4. Create an emotional, motivating, realistic, believeable mind

picture of your prospect successfully using the end result
benefits of your product.

5. Ask a *yes* response trial close question. Immediately upon
getting the prospect's favorable agreement, close the sale.

For example: "Mr. Smith, I understand you are looking for a luxurious two-week cruise (PI) as a gift to your wife (DBM—Love) to
celebrate your 50th wedding anniversary. Is that correct (1)? From
what you have told me, Mr. Smith, I assure you our deluxe four-
teen-day cruise to the Bahamas will do exactly what you want done
(2). Here's an actual picture of the luxurious ship showing in complete detail your accommodations and a schedule of day-to-day
activities, both of which are just what you have requested (3). Just
picture yourself being with your wife on this carefree cruise. It's
your anniversary. You still taste the gourmet food you had for your
anniversary dinner. You dance to the soft music under the stars.
You smell the fresh ocean air. You drink a champagne toast to your
wife. You smile at each other and show your affection. Your wife
thanks you for your thoughtfulness and for the most memorable day
of her life (4). That's just what you want, isn't it (5)? How do you
want your names to appear on your reservations (5)?"

USE SENSUOUS LANGUAGE FOR MAXIMUM
EMOTIONAL APPEAL

IN CREATING A WORD PICTURE, USE CONCRETE LANGUAGE. According
to Webster, *concrete* means "things or events that can be perceived
by the senses: real; actual; not general or abstract." Use one or more
of the five senses of sight, smell, taste, touch, and hearing. Keep it
simple and easy to follow. It must be believeable and tailored for
each prospect. Do not exaggerate. Be brief and do not over-appeal. It
is not necessary to use all five senses. Many times one is sufficient.
Your mind picture should be just long enough to develop a strong
want and a burning desire for your prospect to buy your product.
Your prospect will buy when he or she can *see* himself or herself
successfully using your product.

If you're enthusiastic about the various benefits you have

brought into the mind picture, your prospect will be. If you are not enthusiastic, your prospect won't be. Your enthusiasm will automatically be felt by the prospect to the exact degree you have it. Keep your enthusiasm high.

You've got the creative power it takes to be a dynamic want creator: an imagination. Creating concrete mind pictures will take practice. Make it a habit to use this powerful selling technique in every interview. It's very effective in turning the prospect's need and/or want into a burning desire to own your product. When used properly, this procedure will definitely help you to become an even better champion closer and to close more sales.

THOUGHT-PROVOKING QUOTES

Our main business is not to see what lies dimly at a distance, but to do what lies clearly at hand.
THOMAS CARLYLE

When you are laboring for others, let it be with the same zeal as if it were for yourself.
CONFUCIUS

Of all the many earthly resources we have at our command it is only our minds and the associated unique processes that are truly infinite.
CRAIG DAY

Gnawing on bones of contention provides little nourishment.
ARNOLD GLASOW

Wisdom denotes the pursuing of the best ends by the best means.
FRANCES HUTCHESON

Perhaps the most valuable result of all education is the ability to make yourself do the thing you have to do, when it ought to be done, whether you like it or not.
THOMAS H. HUXLEY

Genius means little more than the faculty of perceiving in an unhabitual way.
WILLIAM JAMES

Happiness is not being pained in body or troubled in mind.
THOMAS JEFFERSON

When a man is in earnest, and knows what he is about, his work is half done.
COMTE DE MIRABEAU

Do what you can, with what you have, where you are.
THEODORE ROOSEVELT

Success or failure in business is caused more by mental attitude even than by mental capacities.

WALTER DILL SCOTT

Education is what survives when what has been learned has been forgotten.

B. F. SKINNER

There is very little difference in people, but that little difference makes a big difference. The little difference is attitude. The big difference is whether it is positive or negative.

CLEMENT STONE

It is not men that interest or disturb me primarily; it is ideas. Ideas live; men die.

WOODROW WILSON

chapter nine

CHAMPION CLOSERS
KNOW WHEN
TO STOP TALKING

Success is not searching for you. You must do
the seeking.
FRANK TYGER

BE READY TO CLOSE ANY TIME

THERE IS ONLY ONE TIME TO CLOSE THE SALE, AND THAT IS WHEN THE PROSPECT IS READY TO BUY. You must be flexible and ready to close the sale at any point—when you are face to face with the prospect, early in your sales talk, halfway through, or late in the interview. Be ready to close any time.

For the top-notch salesperson who is a strong closer, there are many right times to close the sale. For the poor salesperson who is a weak closer, no time is the right time.

THERE IS A RIGHT TIME PERIOD TO ASK
FOR THE ORDER

The very first day I started selling I heard about the famous psychological moment. This is supposed to be the exact one minute in the selling interview when all conditions are right to ask for the order. This thinking is very misleading. It implies that there is just one magic 60-second time span when the sale can be closed.

Granted, it is perhaps possible in the sales presentation that there is just one "moment" to close the sale, but the odds are that there may be two, three, or more times in the interview when the prospect could be closed and each of those times could certainly last more than a minute.

While I do not agree with the psychological moment thinking, I do think there is a right time period when conditions are right to close the sale. It could be a period of one minute, five minutes, thirty minutes, one hour, two hours, a day or even days.

For example, the last time I bought a new boat I saw the exact boat I wanted, but the sales manager was out of town on business for a week. Immediately on his return, we got together and I purchased the boat. The point I am making is that my right time period was one week. I was hot to buy that boat and would have been receptive any time within that seven days.

In another example, my father-in-law looked at a used car. He liked the car very much and wanted to buy it. The owner was out of town until late that afternoon, some six hours after my father-in-law saw the car. Immediately upon the owner's return, my father-in-law purchased the car. His right time period lasted for six hours. He was hot for those six hours, and any time during that time period he could have been sold that automobile.

I mention these examples to make you aware that there is no exact psychological moment, no exact psychological 60-second period.

THE PROSPECT WILL TELL YOU WHEN TO CLOSE

The challenge of knowing when to close is very simple. The prospect will tell you everything you need to know. Professional salespeople are experts at using two very important tools of the trade—trial closes and closing signals. These tools help you to determine how you stand with the buyer. These tools tell you if the buyer is hot, lukewarm, or cold toward your product.

TRIAL CLOSES ARE EFFECTIVE TESTERS

TRIAL CLOSES CAN BE USED ANY TIME, AND YOU'LL NEVER JEOPARDIZE YOUR POSITION WITH YOUR PROSPECT. A trial close is nothing more than an opinion-asking question or a question about some part or function of the product to see if it's acceptable. The answer to your trial close question will tell you how you stand with the prospect. The trial close question is a tester.

For example:

"In your opinion, Mr. Smith, would the smaller, more economical engine be the best for you?"

"In your opinion, Ms. Doe, do you feel that it is worth the added investment of only $35 to have the features of the larger machine?"

"In your opinion, Ms. James, would it be worth sacrificing a bit now so that you could have a worry-free life when you retire?"

"Mr. Ray, is the instrument panel the right height for you?"

"Mr. Smith, you seem to like the yellow color the best; is that correct?"

"In your opinion, Ms. Brown, would this home give you the pride and prestige you are looking for?"

When a positive response is received to your trial close questions, go right to the close without hesitation. A positive response usually indicates that you have gotten yourself an order. If the prospect balks and gives a negative, cold, or lukewarm response, get right back on your sales track, build some more, and try another trial close.

YOU CAN ASK A TRIAL CLOSE QUESTION ANY TIME

You can use a trial close any time and never jeopardize your standing with the prospect. The sharp professional salesperson may use several trial closes in the interview, because he or she knows that it is important to know what the prospect is thinking. The answers to his or her trial close questions help to lead and guide the salesperson toward what has to be done to close the prospect. You must listen carefully and analyze the answers to your questions. You must do some in-depth thinking and make exact, careful interpretations about what the prospect is really telling you.

TRIAL CLOSES HELP YOU TO STAY IN CONTROL

Trial closes have another great advantage. They help you to stay in control of the interview. You control and judge when to ask the questions. The time to ask trial close questions is any time in the interview.

YOU MAY HAVE TO USE TWO, THREE, OR MORE
TRIAL CLOSES

It is possible that you will have to use two, three, or even more trial closes before the actual close is completed. Sometimes you will find that you can't close the prospect after getting a positive response to your trial close question, but try. When you can't close, get right back to selling. Every time you get a positive response to a trial close question you are getting some agreement. Each time you get some agreement you are getting just that much closer to total agreement.

After a negative response is received to a trial close question, immediately get right back to your selling presentation. You've got more work to do. In summary, trial closes are testers that effectively help you to determine exactly how you stand with the prospect.

CLOSING SIGNALS

A CLOSING SIGNAL IS ANYTHING THE PROSPECT SAYS OR DOES THAT INDICATES READINESS TO CLOSE. Keep asking yourself, "Has my prospect mentally bought my product?" Closing signals of acceptance can be put into two categories: vocal (what the prospect says and how it is said) and physical (what the prospect does, how it is done, and how the prospect looks).

VOCAL CLOSING SIGNALS

YOU MUST BE VERY MUCH AWARE OF WHAT THE PROSPECT SAYS, HOW IT IS SAID, AND EXACTLY WHAT IS MEANT. You have to concentrate on what the prospect is saying and completely analyze, with accuracy, everything that is said.

Naturally, when the prospect says, "I'll buy it," that is the clearest of all spoken closing signals. However, I have found very few buyers who come right out and say, "I'll buy it." The prospect may say the same thing, but it comes out altogether differently in the wording.

Again, the key question to ask yourself as your prospect talks is, "Does my prospect mentally own my product?" The prospect

may make a statement or ask a question that will indicate to you that
he or she is ready to close. For example:

"What type of service can I expect?"

"If I buy this now, will I get the additional bonus?"

"Maybe I should wait until you have it on special again."

"If it needs repair work, whom do I call?"

"That sure is a good price for such fine merchandise."

"That's a very fair guarantee."

"I like that red one the best."

"That would go well with my decor."

"Will it last two years?"

Those are all examples of closing signals. When a closing signal is
received, go right to the close, or use a trial close and then go to the
close. Vocal closing signals are strong signals because the prospect
has volunteered a look into his or her mind.

PHYSICAL CLOSING SIGNALS

PHYSICAL CLOSING SIGNALS ARE WHAT THE PROSPECT DOES, HOW IT IS
DONE, AND HOW THE PROSPECT LOOKS. In addition to the vocal closing
signals, prospects many times unconsciously give strong buying
signals by their physical actions. In addition to being a good listener,
you must also be a good observer. Make accurate interpretations
about what the prospect is really telling you.

Some key physical closing signals are when the prospect:

Suddenly becomes friendlier, smiles more, and looks more
relaxed and pleasant. This usually comes from a change in
attitude about you and/or your product.

Appears more interested and suddenly leans toward you.

Picks up the guarantee to read it carefully.

Looks carefully at the label.

Places hands on back of neck.

Places hands together and interlocks fingers.

Looks more alert; eyes start to sparkle.

Begins nodding head in agreement.

Breathes deeply, a sigh of relief.

Studies the literature more closely.

Occasionally, very carefully, examines a sample again; keeps on examining sample.

Picks up order blank and carefully studies any part or all of it.

Opens up tight-fisted hands.

Rubs chin and/or places index finger on cheek.

These are all physical closing signals. The ability to observe and analyze the prospect's actions, gestures, motions, and appearance is as important as being a good listener. When you see these signals in your interview, it is time to take the prospect's temperature with a trial close, or go directly to the close.

ASSUME YOU WILL CLOSE THE SALE—IT'S JUST A MATTER OF WHEN

Assuming you will close the sale should be your attitude when you enter every selling situation. With that attitude, you will realize and be fully aware that it's just a matter of *when* to close the sale.

By perfecting the use of trial closes and vocal and physical closing signals, you will gain additional confidence and never be guilty of overselling the prospect. You'll know when you are in the right time period, and you will be closing sales like a real champion closer.

THOUGHT-PROVOKING QUOTES

Posterity! You will never know how much it cost the present generation to preserve your freedom. I hope you will make good use of it.
JOHN QUINCY ADAMS

The ultimate value of life depends upon awareness and the power of contemplation rather than upon mere survival.
ARISTOTLE

For an idea that does not at first seem insane, there is no hope.
ALBERT EINSTEIN

The ability to think straight, some knowledge of the past, some vision of the future, some skill to do useful service, some urge to fit that service into the well-being of the community—these are the most vital things education must try to produce.
VIRGINIA GILDERSLEEVE

Man must work. That is as certain as the sun. But he may work grudgingly or he may work gratefully; he may work as a man, or he may work as a machine. There is no work so rude that he may not exalt it; no work so impassive that he may not breathe a soul into it; no work so dull that he may not enliven it.
HENRY GILES

Creativity is the act of bringing something new into the world, whether a symphony, a novel, a supermarket, or a new casserole. It is based first on communication with oneself, then testing that communication with experience and reality.
S. I. HAYAKAWA

Discipline does not mean suppression and control, nor is it adjustment to a pattern or an ideology. It means a mind that sees "what is" and learns from "what is."
J. KRISHNAMURTI

It is neither safe nor prudent to do aught against conscience.
MARTIN LUTHER

False conclusions which have been reasoned out are infinitely worse than blind impulse.
HORACE MANN

No one can make a real masterpiece of life until he sees something infinitely greater in his vocation than bread and butter and shelter.
ORISON SWETT MARDEN

Whoever is easily susceptible to the troubles and cares of life is equally susceptible to the joys life has to offer.
HANS MARGOLIUS

Energy and perseverance can fit a man for almost any kind of position.
THEODORE F. MERSELES

Your health is bound to be affected if, day after day, you say the opposite of what you feel, if you grovel before what you dislike, and rejoice at what brings you nothing but misfortune.
BORIS PASTERNAK

The highest regard for man's toil is not what he gets for it, but what he becomes by it.
JOHN RUSKIN

chapter ten

CLOSE THE SALE
LIKE A CHAMPION

To improve the golden moment of opportunity and
catch the good that is within our reach
is the great art of life.
SAMUEL JOHNSON

THE KEYS TO BEING A CHAMPION CLOSER

KEY 1. CHAMPION CLOSERS HAVE THE WILL TO SUCCEED. Champion closers play the game to win. They don't like to lose. They never go at their work in a haphazard, lackadaisical way.

Champion closers have learned to control fear of rejection and fear of failure. No salesperson likes being rejected by the prospect. This is only human. Unless you control fear of rejection, very quickly the fear will develop into dangerous hesitancy and self-doubt, which in turn will automatically be communicated to the prospect. One rejection often leads to one more rejection, and then failure builds on failure. It mushrooms!

FEAR OF REJECTION FEEDS FEAR OF FAILURE. The fear of failure is a powerful motivating force. Salespeople must not let this negative motivating force dominate their professional and personal lives. Fortunately, the will to succeed is likewise a powerful motivating force. The key is to stress in your mind at all times the will to succeed. That positive thinking will overpower the negative fear of failure. You'll never overcome the fear of failure 100 percent. This fear is inside every person. It will always be there, and, as in any competitive situation, the participant has two choices: to win or to lose. The more consciously you keep your goal in mind—will to succeed—the more victories and closes you will have. That is precisely the way to handle your fear of rejection and your fear of failure successfully. Guarantee your success by doing every phase of your selling in a professional, first-rate manner. Success always breeds more success. You can handle your fears by making a habit of winning!

KEY 2. CHAMPION CLOSERS ARE DECISIVE LEADERS. It is impossible to build confidence in your prospect and to help him or her overcome the three basic buyer's fears without having confidence in yourself. Without a confident, leadership-type attitude you are indecisive.

Many buyers are indecisive. How can an indecisive salesperson help an indecisive buyer? When two indecisive people try to make a decision there is no leadership, so nothing positive gets done. When the salesperson is decisive, is positive through strong leadership, and has the power to take charge, he or she can lead the buyer to a favorable close.

KEY 3. CHAMPION CLOSERS NEVER ASSUME THE PROSPECT WON'T BUY. There is no way of knowing, but I am sure we would all be amazed and astonished if somehow we could determine the number of sales lost each day because the salesperson did not ask for the order. In my opinion, salespeople do not ask for the order because they do not expect to get the order. In many of my sales seminars, I occasionally ask for a show of hands in answer to the question, "How many of you, this week, made at least one call on a prospect, assumed that the prospect would not buy, and left without asking for the order?" The percentage always varies, but it runs about 25 to 30 percent.

Logically, there is no reason why you should not get the order. If the salesperson has done a good job of selling the prospect, believes in himself or herself, believes he or she has done his or her best, then the order should be expected.

KEY 4. CHAMPION CLOSERS ARE PERSISTENT—THEY AREN'T AFRAID OF NO'S. Keep on selling and trying to close. It takes lots of courage but it's worth it. Don't give up easily. Make *persistence* a golden word in your vocabulary; make it part of your nervous system; make it a word to govern your actions, a word to work and live by. Don't be a quitter. Don't be afraid of *no*'s. I can't tell you how many *no*'s you should get before you leave the prospect. Every selling situation is different, and you'll have to judge that right on the spot. I have closed many sales after receiving four or five *no*'s. I have also found that the worst prospect a salesperson can be in front of is one who says "yes, yes, yes" all the way through the interview and then says "no" and does not buy.

KEY 5. CHAMPION CLOSERS ASK THE PROSPECT WHO DIDN'T BUY "WHY" AND/OR "WHAT." If all else fails, ask the prospect, "Why didn't you buy?" or "What is there about this product you didn't like?" *Why* is only a three-letter word, but when used properly it can be a sale saver. It is not only an important word going from the prospect's primary interest to find out the dominant buying motive, but *why* is also a very important word to keep you going after a series of *no*'s. *Why* gets the prospect talking again, giving you an opportunity to listen and collect your thoughts, and it gets you back on the right track with the prospect. *Why* has pulled many sales right out of the fire.

After you get several *no* responses from the prospect, ask in a very pleasant, sincere manner, "Why have you decided not to buy?" For example, "Obviously, Ms. Jones, you have a reason for saying *no* to this product. Do you mind if I ask you why you are against going ahead?"

What is likewise a sale saver. It, too, can help you to open up the prospect, find out more important information, and continue selling. For example, "Obviously, Mr. Jones, you have a good reason for not accepting this proposition. Do you mind if I ask you what there is about the product that you dislike?" Many times the prospect will start talking and give you some hidden, deep-down objection or reason that has never been mentioned before. The prospect has done you a real favor by telling you this important information. The prospect has given you another selling opportunity.

KEY 6. CHAMPION CLOSERS KNOW HOW TO SELL AND CLOSE ALL TYPES OF BUYERS. A good salesperson must be able to sell all types of buyers. He or she should be very versatile and able to tailor sales talks to fit every type of prospect. There's the choleric-type buyer, very strong-willed and strong-minded, outspoken, outgoing, who gets what he or she wants at any price. The phlegmatic-type buyer is the quiet, unassuming type, very intelligent, who seldom gets worked up or excited. The sanguine-type buyer is one who sees only the good, is very positive and cheerful, is the eternal optimist. The melancholic-type buyer is constantly negative, always complaining and talking about how bad things are.

To put it another way, there are fast buyers, slow buyers, easy buyers, indecisive buyers, and excessively analytical buyers. The good salesperson will make his or her sales talk fit the type prospect he or she is talking to. The good salesperson keeps in step with the prospect and closes accordingly.

CLOSING TECHNIQUES

CLOSING TECHNIQUES ARE VERY HELPFUL TOOLS TO USE IN SUCCESS-FULLY WRAPPING UP YOUR SALES INTERVIEW, BUT KEEP THEM IN THEIR PROPER PERSPECTIVE. Closing techniques are not meant to take the place of any part of the selling process. In my opinion, for every sale that is lost because of poor closing techniques, there are 50, 100, or even more lost because the salesperson failed to open the prospect's mind, failed to keep the mind open, failed to be convincing, failed in listening, failed in using empathy, failed in arousing burning desire, failed in asking enough questions so that the salesperson knew exactly what the prospect needed and wanted and why the prospect wanted it, and failed to talk intelligently in terms of the prospect's interest.

CLOSING TECHNIQUES ARE TOOLS TO ASSIST YOU TO PROFESSIONALLY BRING YOUR SALES INTERVIEW TO A SUCCESSFUL CONCLUSION. You should have several of the following techniques well in mind, using the one that you feel will best help you to be persuasive with each particular prospect. Be ready to use them in a professional manner on short notice. Constantly assume that you are going to get the order and that you will get a favorable response to these order-asking techniques.

CLOSING TECHNIQUE 1. CHOICE OF TWO OR THE ALTERNATIVE PRO-POSAL. This is very effective. Make it an easy choice. Don't make it involved and compli-cated. You do not ask the prospect *if* he or she is going to buy; you ask the prospect *which* he or she will buy. For example, "Which do you prefer, the solid gold one or the sterling silver one?" or "Which shipping date would work into your production schedule the best—Monday, December 1, or would Friday, December 5 be better?" or "Mr. Smith, did you prefer the 35-inch sleeve length or would you like the 34-inch sleeve length better?"

CLOSING TECHNIQUE 2. THE MINOR POINT. Pick out some minor point and close on that. For example, "Mr. Smith, we can have your shipment out next Monday. Is that satisfactory?" or "Ms. Jones, you want to take advantage of the quantity discount price, don't you?" or "Ms. Doe, we can have your dress ready for you to pick up at 2:00 P.M. tomorrow. Is that satisfactory?"

CLOSING TECHNIQUE 3. THE EXAMPLE CLOSE. Tell an actual, true story of some prospect who had similar interests and what he or she said about your product, how he or she is profitably using it. Emphasize the many benefits he or she is receiving. Make the example relevant to this prospect. If you have used this technique in your conviction, use a different example. Immediately after completing the example, say, "This is what you really want, isn't it?" or "You would like the same thing to happen to you, wouldn't you?"

CLOSING TECHNIQUE 4. ASK HOW THE CUSTOMER'S NAME SHOULD APPEAR ON THE ORDER. "Mr. Jones, did you want your full name to appear on the order or do you use initials?" or "Do you spell your name with two o's or one?" or "I want to make sure that I spell your name correctly. Would you spell it for me, please?"

CLOSING TECHNIQUE 5. THE WEIGH CLOSE. Take a sheet of paper out of your briefcase and draw a line right down the middle of the paper. On one side of the line you put all of the ideas the prospect had against going ahead with your proposition.

On the other side, put all of the benefits the prospect will receive from going ahead at this time. Have many more reasons on the "benefit" side of the paper, the reasons to go ahead. This is called the "weigh close" because the prospect can very easily weigh both sides. It is an effective closing technique. It shows that you are a good salesperson because you have listened to the prospect and have remembered what was said. The key is to make the "benefit" side of the paper "weigh" far more.

CLOSING TECHNIQUE 6. IF I COULD. This closing technique is splendid in helping overcome certain objections. For example: "If I could get the alterations done in time for your meeting Monday, you do want this suit, don't you?" or, "If I could get your shipment on tonight's transport, you do want to place a firm order, don't you?" or, "If I could get the lease on a month-to-month basis, you would go ahead and complete the agreement, right?"

Many times the salesperson is in a good position to negotiate a price between the seller and the buyer, as in real estate and automobile sales. I personally prefer to use this technique only after I have tried some of the other techniques unsuccessfully, making sure that I have some definite agreement with the buyer.

For example, "Mr. Smith, if I could get the seller to lower the price to $125,000, your top dollar according to what you just said, would you then go ahead and complete the purchase agreement?" You and the buyer should have a complete, definite agreement so that you don't run a shuttle service back and forth from the prospect to the seller.

Depending on your product, you may be able to draw up an offer to purchase, putting the details on paper. This technique has saved many sales commissions.

Time is of great importance, so get back to the prospect as quickly as possible to prevent a competitor from stepping in.

CLOSING TECHNIQUE 7. CREATE AN EMOTIONAL PICTURE CLOSE. Even if you have created a vivid, concrete picture of your prospect successfully using the end result benefits of your product just before you asked for the order, another picture or a review of the highlights of the previous picture could certainly help you to arouse more desire and develop more want. Some people have a hard time seeing themselves using something new and foreign to them. Another word picture can help very much in creating stronger desire. Be sure to put right at the close of your picture, "This is really what you want, isn't it, Mary?"

CLOSING TECHNIQUE 8. CUSTOMER LIST. Many salespeople do not use the customer list idea as a mind opener or as evidence to make the prospect feel sure. They save it for the close. It is dynamite! For example, "Jack, here is a partial list of our customers, people who are presently using our product and receiving the many benefits. Don't you agree that it is a very impressive list of names and businesses? [Wait for agreement.] Wouldn't you like to join that select group and start receiving the benefits of our product immediately?"

CLOSING TECHNIQUE 9. SPECIAL OFFER. No gimmicks! It must be aboveboard. Example: "We have fifty mixers left of the current year's model. We are selling them at 25 percent off their original price. When they are gone, there is no way we can get more; that's it. Next year's models are scheduled in later this week. They will sell regularly at 10 percent higher than the price of this year's model, the model we are closing out. You do want to take advantage of the savings, don't you?"

This technique is good for closing the prospect who is not decisive. I caution you not to make it sound like a gimmick. It must be truthful, and you must display high integrity. Don't make it sound like a carnival side show: "Hurry, hurry, we've only got six sets of knives left, first come, first served! Hurry, hurry, hurry, before they are gone! Don't be disappointed!" I know what I say to myself whenever I hear something like that: "That's a con game. I know there are cartons of knife sets left behind the curtain." People resent high-pressure tactics, and rightly so.

CLOSING TECHNIQUE 10. SIMPLY ASK FOR THE ORDER. Timing is important. At the right time, just ask directly for the order. "Ms. Smith, from what you just said, I understand you want to start receiving the benefits of the product as soon as possible. That's correct, isn't it?" or "Mr. Smith, write [or put] your name right here. Your order will be processed immediately."

I suggest that you stay away from asking the customer to "sign right here." Many people are hesitant to "sign" their names, but they will gladly "write" or "put" their names on something.

CLOSING TECHNIQUE 11. SUMMARIZE THE IMPORTANT POINTS. Sometimes when you are in the decision-making process, the prospect forgets some of the really important points. Don't let that happen. Take out a sheet of paper and, as you state some of the important points out loud, write them down. Do this in such a way that the prospect can read the points you have written.

There is magic in writing down all of the important points in front of the prospect's eyes. The prospect can keep glancing at the list as you write and/or talk.

For example, "Joe, I've shown you and told you everything I know about this product and how it will benefit you. Look at the list. It's all here in black and white. This is what you really want, isn't it?"

Always have one or two strong selling points in reserve. Repeat the important points you have discussed thus far and have one or two bonus benefits the prospect will receive which you haven't yet discussed. This makes the prospect feel as though he or she is getting just that much more and your product becomes even more attractive to him or her. I call these extra benefits "sale clinchers."

Use those sale clinchers in your presentation where you may have tried to close twice but without success. You are now ready to try to close for the third time. This time the prospect appears warmer. Step in with the words, "Mr. Doe, in addition to the things I just mentioned and have written down, I neglected to tell you that you will receive a 5-pound box of laundry soap free by purchasing this machine today." Everybody likes to get something extra, something more than what he or she originally planned on receiving.

GETTING THE PROSPECT'S SIGNATURE

IT'S JUST A FORMALITY. "Just put your name there where I put the X, right next to my name," or "Write your name as you want it on the shipping label," or "Please verify the information I have written down," or "Please put your initials right there on the bottom line." Those are all examples of how to ask for the signature. Hand the prospect a pen or pencil and show him or her where the name goes.

Usually sales are closed by verbal buyer agreement before the details are put on the order form. The buyer's signature becomes a mere formality.

Some sales do not require the buyer's signature. Many retail sales or orders given on the telephone do not require a signature. In most cases, however, to make a sales order, contract, or agreement legal and firm, signatures are required.

Perhaps the reason why salespeople are reluctant to ask for the prospect's signature is that they, as well as the prospect, have heard many stories about fast-operating salespeople cheating and defrauding innocent buyers by getting them to sign on the dotted line.

I have found it helpful to get the order form out early in the interview, so that the prospect feels comfortable and is used to seeing it. Then, when it's signature time, I tell the prospect, "Look this over very carefully. Make sure that I haven't made a mistake." The prospect's fears were discussed earlier and, if I have done a good job of selling and have earned the prospect's confidence, there is nothing to fear about getting the prospect's signature.

GETTING THE PROSPECT'S DEPOSIT

ASK FOR IT. Asking for the deposit should not be difficult. Any experienced salesperson will tell you that an order without a deposit is not an order. Leaving your buyer without getting a deposit is asking for a cancellation.

I know one sales manager who made a very striking exhibit out of orders his people brought to him without a deposit. He told his people that an order without a deposit is just like wallpaper on the wall. He actually made a wall full of such orders that were cancelled.

He left them up so that his salespeople could see them again and again to remind them to get a deposit with every order.

Getting money with the order is just the normal way of doing business. When I buy a suit, shirt, typewriter, or car, I expect to pay for the purchase. The buyer will tell you how he or she expects to pay if you will just ask. Getting a deposit is a businesslike way of doing business, and without the deposit the salesperson is open to cancellation.

ONE BRIEF, FINAL, REASSURING COMMENT, "THANK YOU," AND EXIT

You've completed the sales talk. You've gotten the signature on the order. You've gotten the deposit. Many salespeople ask me, "What do I do next?" Two things:

1. CONGRATULATIONS ARE IN ORDER. Congratulate the prospect on his or her wise decision to purchase your product, and reassure the prospect that he or she will receive many longlasting benefits. Make it a brief statement and make it to the point. The prospect will remember your parting words for a long time.

   This technique works very well. It must be a sincere comment right from the heart. This comment can come as you are picking up your papers or putting any exhibit away. "Mr. Smith, I congratulate you on your wise decision to purchase our product. You sure know your merchandise; this is our finest. It will cut down your energy bill just exactly as we discussed, and under this plan you receive ten years of service at absolutely no cost to you. That's our guarantee."

2. A BIG, GENUINE "THANK YOU" AND THEN MAKE YOUR EXIT IMMEDIATELY AND CONFIDENTLY. Show your sincere gratitude. Whether it's a small order or a large one, show your appreciation for the business the prospect has given you and then make your exit.

   I always say, "Hurry, but don't seem hurried." To appear to be rushing would generate suspicion and distrust. You have gotten the order. That was your goal. There is nothing left to talk about.

If you stay longer, you might find yourself in an overkill or oversell situation, which could lead to buyer's remorse and a cancellation.

REVIVING PROSPECTS YOU WERE UNABLE
TO SELL

You've gotten several *no*'s and you have been persistent. Nothing worked. Yet you know a qualified prospect is still a qualified prospect even though you didn't get the order. The prospect has a need for your product, and he or she has the money to buy your product. But you missed.

First, analyze every part of your sales talk and see if you can find out where you went wrong.

Second, ask your manager for ideas and help. The only way for your manager to help you is for you to be completely honest with him or her. Tell your manager exactly what was said and what was not said. Take your manager through what you did and said step by step. As a last resort, if you don't have a manager, talk confidentially to some other professional salesperson you really respect, one whose judgment and wisdom are first-rate and one who is a good closer.

Sometimes you can never figure out what went wrong. I have had selling interviews where it just seemed like nothing made sense to the prospect. Yet I have sold those people at a later date, on the second or third interview.

Here are some effective reviving techniques:

1. Make an even more in-depth study of the prospect and the prospect's needs for your product.

2. Periodically send more testimonial letters, proven statistics, new photographs, and additional sales brochures.

3. Write the prospect a strong sales letter periodically. The letter should contain facts and related buyer's benefits, along with proof (evidence) that ties into his or her primary interest (the need and/or want) and the dominant buying

motive (why it is wanted, if known), thus solving the prospect's problem.

4. Follow up your strong sales letter with a phone call, and try to schedule another appointment. Tell the prospect that you have come up with new, exciting ideas and approaches to help solve his or her problem. (Be ready with the ideas when you get face to face with the prospect!)

Reviving qualified prospects is part of the professional salesperson's job. Don't write off any qualified prospect. Keep the attitude that you'll close the prospect on the next appointment.

The close is the reward for doing a superb job of building the sale. Good closers are good salespeople. Poor closers are poor salespeople. By doing a superb job in all areas of the selling interview, you will receive the highest reward of all to a salesperson, the only thing that counts—the close. Closing techniques are the tools to assist you in professionally bringing your sales interviews to a successful conclusion.

THOUGHT-PROVOKING QUOTES

The first and final thing you have to do in this world is to last in it and not be smashed by it, and it is the same way with your work.
ERNEST HEMINGWAY

Doing little things well is a step toward doing big things better.
HARRY F. BANKS

Think like a man of action, act like a man of thought.
HENRI BERGSON

Real generosity toward the future consists in giving all to what is present.
ALBERT CAMUS

Progress is the mother of problems.
G. K. CHESTERTON

Knowledge is not power by itself. It becomes power only when it is applied.
MARTIN S. DANGLER

Change is inevitable in a progressive country. Change is constant.
BENJAMIN DISRAELI

Creative thinking may mean simply the realization that there's no particular virtue in doing things the way they have always been done.
RUDOLF FLESCH

Don't part company with your ideals. They are anchors in the storm.
ARNOLD GLASOW

To be a great man it is necessary to turn to account all opportunities.
LA ROCHEFOUCAULD

We must ask where we are and whither we are tending.
ABRAHAM LINCOLN

If you choose to work, you will succeed; if you don't, you will fail.
SIDNEY SMITH

Every man has in himself the continent of undiscovered character. Happy is he who acts the Columbus to his own soul.
JAMES STEPHEN

There's more to be feared from closed minds than closed doors.
FRANK TYGER

chapter eleven

OBJECTIONS DON'T MEAN
YOU HAVE LOST
THE SALE

He who cannot change the very fabric of his thought
will never be able to change reality.
ANWAR SADAT

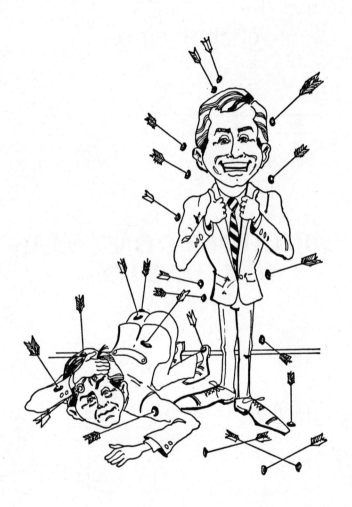

ANSWERING OBJECTIONS PROPERLY IS AN OPPORTUNITY TO BUILD EVEN MORE CONFIDENCE IN YOUR PROSPECT

YOUR ATTITUDE IS A VERY IMPORTANT FACTOR IN HANDLING OBJECTIONS. Some salespeople get angry, irritated, and annoyed when their prospect raises an objection or stalls. They start arguing with the prospect, and the first thing that happens is that the prospect terminates the interview. They have lost the sale because they didn't look at stalls and objections properly.

The way you handle objections, therefore, will do one of two things. It will turn the minus into a plus and build more confidence in the prospect, or it will lose the sale. Promise yourself that you will always stay calm, poised, and collected.

FOCUS YOUR MIND ON WHY OBJECTIONS ARE RAISED

OBJECTIONS AND STALLS USUALLY COME FROM LACK OF KNOWLEDGE AND UNDERSTANDING. The prospect is not clear in his or her mind about a certain point and raises an objection.

Immediately upon getting an objection, ask yourself, "Did I really overcome the buyer's three basic fears? Is this objection really directed at my product, or is it directed toward me?" Try to determine the real reason why the prospect is objecting or stalling.

THE BEST WAY TO LOOK AT AN OBJECTION IS AS A REQUEST FOR MORE INFORMATION. Something is not clear in the prospect's mind, and that, naturally, makes the prospect indecisive. The prospect is really saying, "tell me more; clear up my mind." Once a salesperson realizes the true meaning of objections, then that salesperson's attitude makes him or her glad for objections; objections are good. The prospect has done the salesperson a favor by volunteering that information, getting the information out in the open. Every time the salesperson answers an objection properly, the prospect has even more confidence in him or her.

IT'S OFTEN THE UNSPOKEN OR HIDDEN OBJECTION THAT DEFEATS A SALESPERSON. Many times, the buyer doesn't talk about or express an objection. The sale is lost, and unfortunately the real reason for the loss is never discovered.

Adopt the attitude that objections are good. Realize that the prospect is doing you a favor by bringing information out into the open so that you can clear up his or her mind and build more confidence so that you can close the sale. Don't forget, it's the prospect who agrees with you all the way through who is probably the one you cannot close.

DON'T INTERRUPT THE PROSPECT. BE A GOOD LISTENER. Let the prospect air his or her complete objection before you say a word. Show the consideration of being a sincere good listener. It's tempting to rush in and start talking before the prospect is through, but let him or her finish.

USE EMPATHY MIND CONDITIONERS WHEN YOU START TO ANSWER AN OBJECTION. Don't jump on the prospect. To close the sale success-fully you must develop your ability to change the prospect's think-ing without causing resentment. Use empathy. You are there to win the sale. Say nothing and do nothing that will cause any resent-ment. Maybe you have heard this objection many times, but it is still a problem for the prospect, and it will stay a problem in the pros-pect's mind until it is satisfactorily resolved. Put yourself in your prospect's shoes and see things through his or her eyes. Calmly, confidently, and understandingly answer the objection, starting your reply with an empathy mind conditioner. Some examples follow:

"Mr. Doe, many of our customers felt the same way until I explained . . ."

"I can understand and appreciate your particular concern, Ms. Smith . . ."

"My first reaction was exactly the same as yours, so I really understand how you feel. It wasn't until I considered . . ."

"That's a good question, one that I am frequently asked. I appreciate your interest. I'll be happy to explain it."

"I can see what you mean. Let's take a look at the facts and together we'll determine what they bring out."

"I understand your position, Joe. I'm sorry I didn't bring that point in."

DO AND SAY NOTHING TO PUT THE PROSPECT ON THE DEFENSIVE. Condition your mind so that every time your prospect brings in an objection or a negative statement, you maintain your poise and automatically start your reply with an empathy mind conditioner. Don't use statements like "I can't imagine why you are not interested in . . . ," "I explained that point a few minutes ago . . . ," or "Helen, you usually know quality merchandise, but . . . !" Those kinds of statements put the prospect on the defensive and sell absolutely nothing. Stay in complete control of the interview, and meet the prospect's negative resistance with a relaxed, positive, comfortable, understanding attitude. This will help you to earn the respect and trust of the prospect and earn the prospect's business.

MAKE SURE YOU UNDERSTAND THE OBJECTION. Clarify the prospect's objection by repeating it or asking for it to be repeated. This shows that you are sincerely interested. Make sure there is nothing confusing in the way the objection was asked or in the way you answer the objection.

BE BRIEF. Get to the point quickly. Say just enough and no more to answer the objection satisfactorily. Do not oversell the answer.

TYPES OF OBJECTIONS AND STALLS

A TRUE, GENUINE, BLOCKING OBJECTION. This type of objection must be answered to the prospect's satisfaction or you will never make the sale. To the prospect this is a very honest and legitimate concern.

There will never be a close until the prospect is 100 percent satisfied in his or her mind that all of the concerns have been resolved. You must make the buyer feel sure and confident.

Once you have explained and resolved an objection, the prospect's mind is again open and you are on solid ground. If you can, try to make a selling point out of the objection by turning the objection into a reason (benefit) for buying.

"I'LL HAVE TO THINK IT OVER." This is a stall. Not being able to handle this one satisfactorily has put many salespeople out of the selling profession. The prospect is telling you that he or she is not sold, not convinced. "Let's sit down together, right now, while I am here and can answer all of your questions, and analyze the things you feel you must think over. I'm sorry; apparently I didn't make everything clear."

"I'LL CALL YOU IF I'M INTERESTED." This is another stall. Again the prospect is telling you he or she isn't interested and isn't feeling sure about your product. You must very quickly determine where you went wrong. You have failed to interest the prospect, and you have failed to make the prospect feel sure.

Start asking questions again immediately, verify the primary interest and the dominant buying motive, and then start selling again. Your goal is to convince that buyer that he or she cannot afford to wait.

THE PRICE OBJECTION. "It costs too much," or "The price is too high." When you receive this objection, you have failed to build the value of your product up to equal the price in the prospect's mind. The prospect is saying that from what he or she knows, the product isn't worth what is being asked for it. The best way to handle the price objection is to build your sales-benefits story so well that the price will be offset by the high value of the product. Everything is sold for a price.

I know that sometimes you will have to give the price early in the interview even though you don't want to and you have tried not to. When this happens, immediately try to show how the price is justified by the many benefits your product will bring the buyer.

Most of the times when I was forced to give the price early in the interview, unless I gave a complete sales-benefits talk to justify the price I was never able to make the sale. In other words, don't give the price and then quickly try to justify the price by skipping the entire body of your sales talk and expect to get the order.

MAKE "THE PRICE IS TOO HIGH" WORK FOR YOU. Here's an easy and very effective way to handle this objection. Drop the three-letter word *too*, and make the objection work for you. Make a benefit out of it. "Ms. Smith, the fact that the price is high may be the very reason why you should invest in this high-quality product because [continue on with the related buyer's benefit that fulfills the prospect's primary interest and dominant buying motive]. You do want a very high-quality product that will do these things for you. That's right, isn't it?"

Be sure to drop the word *too*. Otherwise you would be saying that the price is too high or that it does cost too much. Drop the word *too*, and make a good, strong selling point out of the objection by making it a buyer's benefit.

This same technique will work when you get other objections that include the word *too*. For example, "This new adding machine is too complicated," or "This lot is too big." Drop the word *too* and answer these objections as outlined above. As long as the word *too* is in the objection, you have an almost impossible situation to handle.

THE MOLEHILL OBJECTION. This one is tricky. The prospect raises some little objection that may be real or fake, not a true objection at all. Usually this type of objection is small talk and a stall. However, it could be covering up a genuine blocking objection. Sometimes it bears answering and sometimes it does not. You'll have to decide according to the circumstances. If you are selling a very well-to-do person and they say, "I can't afford it," you know that's not a real objection.

If you decide to answer this type of objection, I caution you not to get carried away. I've seen many salespeople try to answer a molehill objection too thoroughly. They start out with a little molehill and before they are through they have made a mountain out of the whole thing and it costs them the sale.

THE HEARSAY OBJECTION. Every salesperson hates to get this objection. Every salesperson has had to handle this one many times. People love to talk and spread rumors. The hearsay objection is something the prospect has heard about you, the product, or your company that is negative in the prospect's mind. It may be true or it may not be true. The prospect believes it. Your job, with all the tact and diplomacy you can use, is to try to make the prospect see the truth. This type of objection is difficult to handle because the prospect has to admit to false thinking, and it isn't easy to him or her to admit a mistake. Negative hearsay objections have a big influence on prospects because they are by nature skeptical of salespeople. Many times the hearsay remarks come from uninterested, uninformed people. The prospect must be turned around or a sale will not be made.

THE IMPOSSIBLE OBJECTION. It's impossible to make something out of nothing. When you are faced, head on, with an impossible objection, it's best to abort the interview and move on to greener pastures. You must decide if it's honestly an impossible objection.

Many times you hear the objection "I can't afford it." In some cases, this is probably true, but in a good many cases the prospect can afford it. It may be a molehill objection, but usually it is a simple excuse or stall that must be handled effectively. Build the value up and make the prospect want your product now. If he or she needs it, make the prospect want it. When you make the prospect really *want* what he or she *needs*, you'll close the sale. If you are convinced there is no money there, move on.

Another objection is "I don't need it." You must determine if it is or is not needed. You can't sell milking machines to someone who doesn't have cows. If the prospect truly doesn't need it, move on to a qualified prospect. Do not overlook the fact that the prospect could be covering up a product or price objection.

DIG DEEPLY AND FORCE OUT HIDDEN OBJECTIONS

WHEN ALL ELSE FAILS, TRY THESE SIX MAGIC QUESTIONS. You've asked for the order several times and failed to get a positive response. You feel that you have answered all of the objections properly. Then try the steps outlined below. Perhaps you will have to use only the first three steps to get the real objection. Use as many of the following steps in sequence as are necessary for you for force out the hidden objection.

1. A *why* question: "Obviously, you must have some good reason for saying that. Do you mind if I ask what it is?"

2. "In addition to that, is there any other reason why you would hesitate?"

3. Meet the condition: "If I could show you that [your product will do what the prospect wants done] then you would buy now. Isn't that right?"

4. "Obviously, there is some other reason why you are hesitating. Do you mind if I ask what it is?"

5. Bury previous objections: "Oh, it wasn't the . . . then that concerned you, was it?" Go back to questions 2, 3, and 4 as often as needed until you are satisfied that you have finally gotten the real reason out in the open.

6. "Then it boils down to this: [restate the objection]. Is that the real question?" Then go ahead and answer this objection with more evidence, additional benefits, motivational selling, and so on.

This sequence of six points is an excellent way to dig deeply and to force out the hidden objection.

ANSWER OBJECTIONS AS SOON AS POSSIBLE

The sooner an objection is answered to the satisfaction of the prospect, the better. Once it is properly answered, the sales talk can be started again, full speed ahead. Don't put off answering an objection unless you have a very good reason. If you are going to conduct a demonstration or use some type of exhibit later in the interview that would help you to answer the objection, acknowledge it when it is brought up and explain to the prospect that you will make further explanation when you conduct your demo. Be sure to handle it at that time.

As you experience various objections in your selling interviews, try to work the answers into your regular sales track. This keeps the objections from ever being brought up.

DON'T BE AFRAID OF OBJECTIONS

WHEN THE PROSPECT RAISES AN OBJECTION, LISTEN BETWEEN THE LINES. What the prospect really means by what he or she is saying is vital. It determines what you say and do to close the sale. Use empathy mind conditioners when you start to answer an objection. Be calm, confident, positive, and understanding, and you will build even more confidence in your prospect. Always ask for the order or use a trial close after you have answered an objection.

THOUGHT-PROVOKING QUOTES

The only way to achieve true success is to express yourself completely in service to society.

ARISTOTLE

If there's no one else better than yourself, you haven't looked hard for someone else . . . and haven't looked hard at yourself.

ROBERT HALF

Many ideas grow better when transplanted into another mind than in the one where they sprang up.

OLIVER WENDELL HOLMES JR.

Statesmanship is the art of knowing and leading the multitude, or the majority. Its glory is to lead them, not where they want to go, but where they ought to go.

JOSEPH JOUBERT

Don't be discouraged by a failure. It can be a positive experience. Failure is, in a sense, the highway to success, inasmuch as every discovery of what is false leads us to seek earnestly after what is true, and every fresh experience points out some form of error which we shall afterwards carefully avoid.

JOHN KEATS

Ambition and suspicion always go together.

GEORG C. LICHTENBERG

A great man is made up of qualities that meet or make great occasions.

JAMES RUSSELL LOWELL

It is good to think well; it is divine to act well.

HORACE MANN

The more freedom a man has, the more important it is that he be a responsible man.
RAYMOND RUBICAM

The best reformers the world has ever seen are those who commence on themselves.
GEORGE BERNARD SHAW

Some persons do first, think afterward, and then repent forever.
THOMAS SECKER

If you cannot lift the load off another's back, do not walk away. Try to lighten it.
FRANK TYGER

Man is not on the earth solely for his own happiness. He is there to realize great things for humanity.
VINCENT VAN GOGH

Wealth is not acquired, as many persons suppose, by fortunate speculations and splendid enterprises, but the daily practice of industry, frugality and economy. He who relies upon these means will rarely be found destitute, and he who relies upon any other will generally become bankrupt.
FRANCIS WAYLAND

chapter twelve

GOOD CLOSERS KNOW WHERE THEY ARE GOING AND COLLECT BIG DIVIDENDS FROM TIME AND GOOD WORKING HABITS

The great law of culture: Let each become all that he was created capable of being.
THOMAS CARLYLE

ESTABLISH A TRACK TO YOUR DESTINATION

WHERE DO YOU WANT TO GO? Tryon Edwards said, "Thoughts lead on to purposes; purposes go forth into action; actions form habits; habits decide character; and character fixes destiny."

Very recently I was conducting a sales seminar for a company in New York. I asked the question, "How many of you have written out your goals?" The results were stunning, yet the percentages run the same all over the country. There were 123 salespeople present, and only three responded positively that they had written out their goals. That's alarming!

PROPER GOAL SETTING AND GOOD EXECUTION OF GOALS AUTOMATI-CALLY SOLVES MANY IMPORTANT PROBLEMS FOR SALESPEOPLE. Once the goals have been set and put into positive action the salesperson is automatically becoming well organized and doing things in the order of their importance; that salesperson also is developing good working habits and becoming a good self-disciplined individual.

The goal-minded salesperson never takes his or her mind off the long-range goals, because that salesperson knows the penalty—the short-term frustrations come in and wipe you out. It is so simple to set goals and establish a positive track to run on, and yet 95 percent of salespeople today are working without any plan to follow. They are merely going this way one day and that way the next day, with no exact target in mind. It's as impossible to hit something you have never seen (target) as it is to come back from someplace you have never been!

William Jennings Bryan made an outstanding statement about goals and destiny: "Destiny is not a matter of chance, it is a matter of choice; it is not a thing to be waited for, it is a thing to be achieved."

When you have no goal to be really interested in and committed to, you go around in circles feeling lost and feeling that life and your profession are purposeless. People who say that life is not worthwhile are really saying that they have no personal or job goals that are worthwhile. Goals should be realistic, personal, and worthy; something that justifies extra effort; something really worth working for; something you will be proud of when you accomplish them successfully.

ACCURATELY AND HONESTLY DETERMINE YOUR PRESENT SITUATION. You must know exactly where you are now, your present situation, and where you want to go, your future situation. *Know thyself.* Look at yourself honestly and squarely. Ask, "What do I want to do and what do I want to be? Do I want a promotion? Do I want a business of my own? What are my resources? Do I want to change fields? What do I have to do to get there? What are my strengths and what are my weaknesses? How much money do I want to make? What do I want to provide my family . . . home, education, car, vacation, insurance?" Make a complete list and study all of the facts.

SET AND DEFINE YOUR REALISTIC, WORTHY GOALS. Use crystallized thinking. From your list, decide on your overall major goal. Aim high and have great expectations. The very minute you write out your goals, dedicate yourself to their successful attainment. Constantly think and imagine yourself succeeding, thus crowding out any negative, fearful thoughts. Dress and act the part of the successful salesperson you really want to be. Always work and live by unconquerable faith, and be persistent. Persistence always develops purpose, direction, and courage.

DEVELOP A COMPLETE PLAN OF SPECIFIC ACTIVITIES. Think and determine how you are going to accomplish your major and sustaining goals. Develop a complete plan of specific activities, what has to be done and how it is going to be done. Leave nothing to chance. Every point must be clearly defined on an hour-to-hour basis, day-to-day basis, week-to-week basis, month-to-month basis. Major goals are accomplished by completing the sustaining goals one at a time. Your selling day will be one of organized activity. Visualize in your mind the successful completion of every sustaining goal.

Go at every activity without giving thought to the possibility of defeat. Concentrate on your strengths and not on your weaknesses. Be determined to follow through on every point in your goal achievement plan. This develops even more self-confidence and faith in your abilities and helps you to conquer obstacles and circumstances that might get in your way. Develop a burning desire for successful accomplishment of your goals. A true, heartfelt, burning desire is the most powerful motivator there is.

TIMETABLES STOP PROCRASTINATION. Timetables and deadlines are very important. When do you want to achieve these goals? Don't use terms like "a long time," "shortly," "about two years," "some time in the future," or "possibly six months." Write down the actual dates you want these goals to be a reality. Every date should be specific, nothing general, nothing fuzzy. This stops procrastination and provides you with checking points.

Stop and think. What are you really doing when you write out and set your goals? You are turning intentions into commitments, commitments into involvements, involvements into positive actions. Goals stop drifting. Remember—no purpose, no progress.

Goals also make you think your way to success, make you aware of your great potential, and help you to stay motivated to peak performance. When you are really motivated, obstacles never stop you. You find a way to overcome problems and challenges. Happiness and accomplishment are the results of overcoming obstacles on your way to achieving realistic, big goals.

THE THREE QUALITIES THAT MAKE GOALS DYNAMIC

1. GOALS ARE CONCRETE. Concrete goals are characterized by things or events that can be perceived by the senses. They are real, actual, particular, and specific. They are not general or abstract. Concrete goals produce positive action.

2. GOALS PROVIDE A YARDSTICK. Goals are measurable, allowing you to determine and to judge your progress.

3. GOALS ARE TIME TARGETS. Goals also help you to measure progress in terms of time. Time targets provide a schedule to make sure not only that things are happening for you but also that things are happening within a certain time period. Deadlines give you an

exact checking point to make sure your major and sustaining goals are being accomplished as planned and as scheduled.

A SIMPLE GOAL OUTLINE THAT NEVER FAILS

DEVELOP A COMPLETE GOAL BLUEPRINT USING THE GOAL OUTLINE. Everyone's circumstances are different, so there is no way that I can fill out your form for you. This is just a sample to illustrate the procedure. Take time right now to build yourself a complete goal outline. You will have your overall major goal. You may have ten to fifteen (or more) sustaining goals, and for each sustaining goal you may have from five to fifteen (or more) specific activities that must be accomplished.

MAJOR GOAL

I will have done an outstanding job for the next calendar year by increasing my sales commissions or achieving a promotion to [title], so that my total income will be X number of dollars. Then, each year thereafter, I will increase my income to X number of dollars over the previous year. This will enable me to purchase [item] by [date], [item] by [date], [item] by [date], [item] by [date], [item] by [date], [item] by [date].

Sustaining Goal 1.

To maintain an adequate number of bona fide prospects to keep me busy and selling productively all day, every day.

SPECIFIC ACTIVITIES to do daily, weekly, monthly.

1. Devote a minimum of four hours per week to productive prospecting.
2. Develop and maintain close contact with productive centers of influence.
3. Get leads from every person I sell.

4. Get favorable PR by speaking to one service club, church group, or company meeting per month.

5. Prospect at least two hours per week using the telephone. Use the telephone or person-to-person contact to call on five present customers and ask each for names of prospects.

Sustaining Goal 2.

Make X number of face-to-face presentations monthly.

SPECIFIC ACTIVITIES to do daily, weekly, monthly.

1. Fill each day with X number of productive appointments.
2. Fill each week with X number of productive appointments.
3. Be in the field making calls during X number of hours daily, weekly.
4. Do necessary paper work during nonproductive calling hours.
5. Have available more than an adequate number of bona fide prospects each day.
6. Preselect each day alternate cold calls to fill in any open time.
7. Make X number of face-to-face presentations daily, weekly.

Sustaining Goal 3.

Increase the ratio of sales closings.

SPECIFIC ACTIVITIES to do daily, weekly, monthly.

1. Analyze each attempt to sell.
2. Read a book on selling X number of minutes per day.
3. Listen to cassette tapes between calls.
4. Review and study company sales-training methods X number of times weekly.
5. Set up a definite self-improvement program.

Sustaining Goal 4.

Make most productive use of time.

SPECIFIC ACTIVITIES to do daily, weekly, monthly.

1. Every evening plan for best utilization of time for next day.
2. Utilize phone to firm up all appointments each day.
3. Visit less and spend more time selling on each interview.
4. Permit no nonproductive use of time during prime selling hours.
5. Daily, weekly, and monthly do things in the order of their importance.
6. Arrange appointments from a geographical standpoint.

Sustaining Goal 5.

Maintain a positive, enthusiastic attitude.

SPECIFIC ACTIVITIES to do daily, weekly, monthly.

1. Use X number of pep talks daily.
2. Read one good book on self-improvement every month.
3. Listen daily to inspirational tapes.
4. Keep my mind on the importance of achieving my goals.
5. Be an example of an enthusiastic person.
6. Review my goals daily.

THIS IS ONLY A SMALL SAMPLE OF HOW TO COMPLETE YOUR GOAL SETTING. You may have fifteen or more sustaining goals and fifteen or more specific activities to do in order to accomplish each sustaining goal. To complete this form requires much concentrated thought, but I assure you it will be worth it. Once you see your goals in your mind and believe it in your heart, you will achieve it.

PUT EVERY DETAIL OF YOUR GOAL OUTLINE INTO ACTION IMMEDIATELY

NONE OF THE ABOVE WILL DO YOU ANY GOOD UNLESS IT IS PUT INTO ACTION IMMEDIATELY. Make a firm commitment to yourself that every single part of your goals will be put into action as of a specific date and time.

MAKE REGULAR CHECKUPS

PROFESSIONAL SALESPEOPLE KNOW THE IMPORTANCE OF FOLLOW-UP. I suggest that you check up on your progress at least once a week. Small deviations will show up, and they can be corrected before they become big problems. These problems could block and delay your goal achievements. A checkup doesn't take much time, but it is time well spent; you will know exactly what you have done right and exactly what you have done wrong. Self-analysis is the key to growth as well as the vital key to goal achievement.

SUCCESSFUL GOAL ESTABLISHMENT EQUALS GOOD TIME MANAGEMENT

When you have done a good job of setting your goals by the above method, you have automatically licked the problem of time management and of getting yourself organized. Lack of organization and not using time wisely is the second biggest failure of salespeople. By going through every step of the goal-setting process as I have recommended, you will always be well organized and will always be carrying out your activities in the order of their importance. You will rapidly reap the great benefits of being a goal-oriented salesperson instead of a task-oriented salesperson. There's a big difference!!

THOUGHT-PROVOKING QUOTES

The ideal man bears the accidents of life with dignity and grace, making the best of circumstances.

ARISTOTLE

Immense power is acquired by assuring yourself in your secret reveries that you were born to control affairs.

ANDREW CARNEGIE

Learning without thought is labor lost. Thought without learning is intellectual death.

CONFUCIUS

The growth of the human mind is still high adventure, in many ways the highest adventure on earth.

NORMAN COUSINS

It is easier to enrich ourselves with a thousand virtues than to correct ourselves of a single fault.

JEAN DE LA BRUYÈRE

Failure is instructive. The person who really thinks learns quite as much from his failures as from his successes.

JOHN DEWEY

Difficulties exist to be surmounted.

RALPH WALDO EMERSON

Coming together is a beginning; keeping together is progress; working together is success.

HENRY FORD

He cannot be good that knows not why he is good.

THOMAS FULLER

Success is simple. Do what's right, the right way, at the right time.

ARNOLD GLASOW

No man knows how bad he is until he has tried very hard to be good.

C. S. LEWIS

Man's chief purpose is to live . . . not to exist. I shall not waste my days trying to prolong them. I shall use my time.

JACK LONDON

What is defeat? Nothing but education; nothing but the first step to something better.

WENDELL PHILLIPS

The great difficulty in education is to get experience out of ideas.

GEORGE SANTAYANA

chapter thirteen

EFFECTIVE PROSPECTING AND TELEPHONING YOUR WAY TO MORE PROFITS

Fear of self is the greatest of all terrors, the deepest of all dread, the commonest of all mistakes. From it grows failure. Because of it, life is a mockery. Out of it comes despair.
DAVID SEABURY

EFFECTIVE PROSPECTING AND TELEPHONING

ALWAYS GO HUNTING WHERE THE DUCKS ARE. On a very cold November morning I crawled out of bed at 4:00 A.M. to go duck hunting with my father. Little did I realize that I would learn a tremendous lesson about prospecting in the sales profession. At that time I was still in college, and my life's profession was as yet undecided. The temperature was down to zero that morning, and it was still very dark as we made our way across the Platte River to our duck blind.

Once we reached the blind we realized that there was very little open water in which to place our decoys; everything was pretty well frozen over. We listened, and in an area about one-fourth of a mile from where we were, we could hear ducks by the dozen, quacking away. There was a hot hole there where the water didn't freeze.

We made our way to the hot hole in the dark, crawling the last few feet and being as quiet as we could. We were right. The ducks were there by the hundreds. We lay on that cold ground until the sun started to come up and we could legally fire our guns. The firing time arrived, and in a matter of ten seconds we had both emptied our guns at the ducks. We scored. Each of us had our limit of ducks in a matter of seconds, something that probably would have taken all morning had we stayed at the blind; or, perhaps, in that blind we wouldn't have shot any ducks at all.

My point is this: We accomplished in ten seconds, by putting forth extra effort to get to where the ducks were, as much or maybe far more than if we would have stayed in the blind all day waiting for the ducks to come to us. In prospecting, always go to where the ducks (prospects) are. Don't wait for the prospects to come to you. Don't wait for things to happen to you; get out and make them happen *for* you.

DEVELOP A POSITIVE PROSPECTING SPIRIT

EFFECTIVE PROSPECTING IS YOUR KEY TO GROWTH. Every successful salesperson knows that he or she must get the story told to the most qualified people at the lowest possible expense to make his or her time pay the biggest dividends. The key question to ask yourself is, "Could I be making higher commissions and, at the same time, spend less money and time getting my story in front of qualified prospects?" That question should be on your mind constantly and with priority.

If you have set your goals, as I discussed in the last chapter, you are setting aside a certain amount of time daily, weekly, or monthly for prospecting. That time must pay dividends. You can't sell someone you cannot see. If you don't prospect profitably, your goals will never become reality. Without qualified prospects, your selling time becomes frustrating and all doors and minds seem to be closed. You are dead-ended.

ELIMINATE WASTED TIME. Many salespeople spend more time in their automobiles than they do seeing people. Most salespeople are only employed when they are face to face with a prospect, and that amount of time is very short. It will vary some, of course, but the average salesperson is in front of or in contact with a prospect only about two hours per day.

Proper prospecting can cut down on wasted driving time. Salespeople waste much time running down nonqualified prospects. Many salespeople make unplanned calls on prospects either at their offices or in their homes, and many times those prospects are not in or will not see a salesperson.

When the prospect will not see you once you are there, or if the prospect isn't there, that's wasted time. Those trips and nonselling activities, such as waiting in offices or homes to see the prospect, consume a great part of every salesperson's working day. There is actually very little time left and very little time spent on productively prospecting and selling.

CUT DOWN ON WASTED AUTO EXPENSES. Driving a car today with no definite place to go not only wastes time, but it also wastes a lot of money. Keep accurate records of prospecting time used for each prospect, and also keep a record of prospecting expense for each prospect. Constantly try to lower time and expense per prospect.

TWO TYPES OF PROSPECTS

DEFINE WHAT A QUALIFIED PROSPECT REALLY IS. I define a qualified prospect as one who has the ability to buy and who knowingly or unknowingly has a need or want for your product.

Naturally, your prospecting efforts will be directed first toward finding the prospects who have the ability to buy and knowingly have the need for your product.

Next you will want to locate those prospects who have the ability to buy but do not realize that they have a need for your product. They do not know what your product is and what it can and will do for them.

WHERE TO FIND PROSPECTS

THOSE WHO ARE BUYING FROM YOU NOW. Your present customers, who are now buying from you, are naturally the choicest of all prospects. You can sell them more of the present product; you can sell them other products in your line; you can sell them add-ons; you can sell them on expanding and giving your products more shelf and/or display space. Customer acceptance of you, your company, and your product is very beneficial, as it usually means more sales in the future.

REFERRALS FROM PRESENT CUSTOMERS ARE ALSO A GREAT SOURCE. Customers who are happy and satisfied will know and recommend others they feel will benefit from buying from you. But you must ask for the referrals. As with closing the sale, you must ask for the order. The same is true in getting referrals. Ask for them. Stay in contact with those who have bought from you. Phone or write "thank you's." Be the rare salesperson who, a few days or weeks after the sale, phones the customer to make sure the purchase is working out.

Keep building your customers and take a sincere "I care about you'' interest in them. They'll appreciate you very much. Very few salespeople do this. Of the many household appliances, automobiles, lawn mowers, and insurance policies that my wife and I have purchased in the last five years, I have not received *one* follow-up call from a salesperson! I'll bet you have had the same experience.

I know of no better way to sell new prospects and to open up new business than by way of a mutual friend making a referral. The method used in meeting the new prospect should be thought out. Is it possible for the customer to introduce you personally? If not, perhaps he or she could write the prospect a short letter introducing you or make a phone call to do so.

Remember, your present customer has a great amount of faith and confidence in you, and you want to transfer that feeling to the new prospect and be well accepted. The way you are first accepted is very important and will usually determine whether or not the sale is closed successfully.

Follow-up should be included as part of your goal plan. You'll get many qualified referrals from this source.

ASK THE PERSON WHO HAS JUST BOUGHT. This is another great source of prospects. Even though, at this point, they haven't used the product, they are excited about the product and are expecting great things. They are happy with you. Ask for the names of two or three prospects right after the order is signed. If the prospect you just sold is an influential person, make doubly certain that you ask for referrals. Better yet, ask the prospect to call while you are there and introduce you on the phone to a friend. Many times, the influential leader can even set up the appointment for you.

Say something like this: "Ms. Jones, I am extremely happy that we could get together today and talk about some of your problem areas. Congratulations to you on the wise decision to purchase this product. I know that you will be very happy with the results as they will definitely solve the particular problems for you that we discussed. I will follow up and make sure you receive the product right on schedule, and I will also make sure that it is performing to your satisfaction.

"Ms. Jones, if you feel you can do so, I would appreciate the names of two or three people you feel would like the benefits of my product and who would be qualified buyers. In contacting them, I will use your name only if you want me to."

I always ask for two or three names. One sounds too few and, on the other hand, more than two or three sounds like too many. If the prospect knows more than two or three prospects, he or she usually will volunteer that information.

Using an effective approach like this at the right time should make referrals an endless source of qualified prospects.

FORMER CUSTOMERS. Many times, after some cultivation of proper exposure, phone calls, direct mail, and a direct approach, former customers are good prospects. They were sold once. Given time and the right approach, many of these people are good prospects. You'll have to resolve the reason why they discontinued doing business with you and/or your company. It is always an interesting challenge, but for the real human engineer this source can be very productive.

COMPETITIVE CUSTOMERS. It seems that people who buy from competitors are the world's worst prospects. Many other salespeople I have talked to feel the same way. I have also found out that when you quit being allergic to repeated rejections, they are choice prospects because they have the ability to buy and they have the need for your product. It takes some time, persistence, and lots of follow-up with effective direct mail and telephone calls, but many of these prospects can be sold.

FAMILY AND FRIENDS. This can be a good source, depending, of course, on what your product is.

THE PERSON WHO HAS JUST TURNED YOU DOWN. Many times the person who has just turned you down was not a qualified buyer; maybe the timing was bad; but regardless of the reason for the turndown, I still make it a point to ask for referrals.

ADVERTISING IN NEWSPAPERS AND PERIODICALS; ON RADIO AND TELEVISION. Depending on your product, leads often can be obtained by using newspapers, periodicals, radio, and television. Many companies generate leads from these sources for their salespeople. Sometimes the salespeople must do this for themselves. Coupon responses are another source. The effectiveness will vary from product to product. Sometimes you may find good leads; other times just the names and addresses of lookers or people who just bought a competitor's brand; and some will be people who have no interest at all. The only way you can find out how good they are is to qualify them. The phone works best for that.

DIRECT MAIL. This source can be very effective in producing leads. Testing is vital. Logically, direct mail should be much better than the average run of the mill from general advertising, because it is directed toward prospects who have bought a product similar to yours or to prospects who have a need. Direct mail can be an excellent source of uncovering qualified buyers.

The key to handling any type of advertising leads is to do it quickly and efficiently, getting to the qualified prospects before your competitor does, and getting to them while they are still hot.

SPECIAL PROMOTIONS AND TRADE SHOW EXHIBITS. There are many lookers who attend things like show booths, but this can be an excellent source for prospecting. Many serious buyers attend shows and promotions to help themselves make the right decision about products and to see what is available. Guest books and names on free drawing cards will produce many who are "just looking," but they will also produce some serious, well-qualified prospects who attend to find the solutions to their particular problem.

PUBLISHED MATERIALS. In this day and age, there are many published directories, periodicals, and other data collections available. Some are easy to obtain. Other information you will have to search to find. You will find much-needed information in business sections of local newspapers; business newspapers; periodicals published by the Chamber of Commerce, various service clubs, and professional organizations; or weekly church bulletins. Watch for company personnel changes, new product releases, people moving in and out, people being promoted, company functions, latest news about your customers and prospects, news about your competitors, people serving on various community fund drives, or those who have recently joined various organizations. New businesses starting or those expanding can be excellent sources. The list is endless.

USE THE LIBRARY. Ask the librarian to assist you in finding the information you need. You'll be surprised at how much vital information is contained in your library and how willing librarians are to assist you. The phone book is valuable, as are the many companies that specialize in furnishing mailing lists covering specific prospects. In fact, with so many sources available in which to find prospects, a salesperson should be kept busy every minute of the selling day.

COLD CALLS. I have always felt that it is best to have a firm appointment if you can do so, because you have qualified your prospect and the prospect is expecting you. You have started to build a sale, and that means a lot. But don't sell cold calling short. You can drop the salesperson who can handle cold calls into any city in this country, and that salesperson will always do very well. That type of salesperson makes every second of the day pay dividends. It takes courage, but it certainly pays off.

When you have time between scheduled calls, have an appointment cancelled on short notice, or have a no-show situation, don't allow that time to be dead time. Make it profitable by cold calling. It is a very secure feeling to know that when things go wrong you can handle the situation by filling the time with profitable actions.

BUILD A PROSPECT FILE. While you are active in the field, you will hear the names of people who are possible prospects. Write down all the information you can, preferably on index cards. This file is just like having an insurance policy. It pays off when you need it. Whenever you are faced with a cancellation or no-show, the prospect file can save the day, just like cold calling. It's just another tool to help make prime selling time pay dividends.

THE TELEPHONE IS VERY VALUABLE

THE SHORTEST DISTANCE BETWEEN YOU AND YOUR PROSPECT IS NOT A STRAIGHT LINE, BUT THE TELEPHONE LINE. The telephone, when properly used, can be very valuable in helping you to achieve your selling goals. It can be an excellent way to make your first contact. Some of the telephone's greatest benefits are:

1. It enables you to contact the greatest number of prospects in the shortest period of time. You can do in thirty minutes on the phone what would take several days to do driving from prospect to prospect.

2. It saves wasted auto time and driving expense.

3. It enables you to qualify your prospects, so that you aren't wasting your time on hopeless, nonqualified prospects.

4. It enables you to plan your day efficiently and organize your time. Prospects can be placed in a logical, well-thought-out, geographical order.

5. It conditions the prospect's mind and starts the prospect thinking about you and your product's benefits. Thus, you are not barging in on the spur of the moment, taking the prospect by surprise, or disrupting the prospect's schedule and/or activities. It makes you look very businesslike and professional. It lets the prospect know you really respect him or her and his or her schedule.

6. It enables you to set up a definite appointment time that both you and the prospect can work around; thus, it eliminates excessive wasted time in the office or home because the prospect is busy doing something else and doesn't want to quit in the middle of the project.

7. It is an ice breaker, and it gives you an opportunity to make a very relaxed, sincere first impression. It also helps you to be more relaxed when following up and calling on the prospect at the appointment time, as you know he or she is expecting you and has agreed to meet you.

8. It enables you to make sure that all interested people who will be involved in the decision will be present. This saves a call back or being told that they would pass your sales message along to the other decision makers (which usually just doesn't happen), costing you the sale.

9. It enables you, if your product or service is right, to close the sale. Because most products do not fall into this category, the material presented here is all geared for selling the interview.

10. It enables you to start building a strong sales foundation with the prospect. Listen carefully and analyze the prospect. Many times clues are dropped, enabling you to build an even stronger face-to-face interview.

With so many good reasons for using the telephone to help you prospect more effectively, don't ignore this valuable tool. My work shows that there are two basic reasons why salespeople do not use the phone. The first is fear. They are afraid of being rejected and afraid of getting a *no* response. Once you have telephoning techniques down pat for obtaining the interview, you will welcome a *no* response or indication of lack of interest because it eliminates your wasting good time on people who are not qualified prospects. Second, salespeople lack effective telephone techniques and know-how. Once they develop the know-how, confidence replaces fear.

YOUR GOAL FOR USING THE PHONE. Keep your mind on your goal for using the phone, and that goal should be to find qualified, prospective buyers with whom you can arrange personal interviews under favorable circumstances. When phoning, never get trapped into trying to sell your product, unless you have the unique product or situation that you can close right then. Keep your mind on one thing—selling the appointment, the interview. Sometimes the prospect will question you about yourself and your product, perhaps about your company, but remember, the more selling of the product you do on the phone, the less chance you will have for the interview.

Stay in control. Don't bend toward the temptation of selling the product on the phone. Give just enough mind-opening statements to persuade the prospect to make a favorable interview decision. You may want to ask a few questions to determine if the prospect really is a prospect and if the scheduling of an appointment is worthwhile.

DEVELOP A SHORT, BRIEF TELEPHONE TRACK. Here is a model telephone outline for making appointments. Make notes and have them right beside you when you first start out. Get the format and your material well organized in your mind as soon as possible. Having the material in mind and well organized will help you to build and radiate more confidence, and it will make you feel very comfortable.

1. State name of prospect.
2. Introduce yourself.
3. Repeat name of prospect.
4. Use a well-planned approach. State your purpose in calling. This should be a mind-opening statement, filled with ideas and benefits. Use just enough to convince the prospect that an appointment is justified.
5. Request adequate time for face-to-face interview. Don't ask for ten minutes if you know you'll need thirty.
6. Ask for appointment. Set time and location, and get all necessary people there. Make it seem important. Give thought to the prospect's best free time. It is best to see office and production workers at home. Many companies understandably do not want people taken off their jobs for sales talks. Physicians and dentists usually can be seen during office hours, but make sure that you know what those hours are. Try to determine in advance the best time to see them. Attorneys usually can be seen after court hours, and investment and stockbrokers after the market closes. Traveling people usually prefer Saturday mornings, but that would be the worst time to see merchants. Sometimes teachers can be seen after classes, sometimes between classes, and sometimes on Saturday mornings. Homemakers usually prefer midmorning or midafternoon, but it is best to have them tell you the time they prefer. Picking out the most convenient time for the prospect is very important, as you do not want to get halfway through the interview and then have your prospect announce that he or she must get back to work and cannot see you any longer that day. Luncheon appointments can be ideal for hard-to-see people. Tips on luncheon appointments appear below.

The following is an example:

"Good morning, Mr. Jones (1)."

"This is E. J. Smith speaking. I am with the XYZ Company (2)."

"Mr. Jones (3), recently my company came up with an exciting idea and a unique savings and investment plan that could possibly save you a lot of time, trouble, and an unnecessary loss of money in building your carefree retirement (4)."

"It would take me about twenty minutes to show you this new idea and to determine how beneficial it could be to you (5)."

"Which time would be better for you—Monday at 10:00 A.M., or would Tuesday at 3:00 P.M. be more convenient? (6)"

If the prospect says he or she isn't interested, try something like this: "Of course, you aren't interested. If you were interested, you would have already called us or some other good, reliable company." Then, immediately go back and state the benefits of your idea and what it means to him or her.

You might want to try a question right at the end of number 4: "You are interested in saving time, trouble, and an unnecessary loss of money in setting up your carefree retirement program, aren't you?"

If it is a referral, use something like this: "Our mutual friend, Jack Johnson, suggested I contact you. Recently we were able to help Jack save a great amount of time, trouble, and an unnecessary loss of money in setting up a unique savings and investment program that will provide him with a carefree retirement. Jack thought you might be interested in this new idea."

LUNCHEON APPOINTMENTS CAN BE IDEAL. When a few simple rules are followed, luncheon appointments can be extremely helpful. If you feel that the prospect is going to be interrupted with employees, associates, the telephone, or visitors, invite him or her to have lunch with you. You must make circumstances right or you will never

close the sale. You want the prospect's undivided and uninter-
rupted attention.

Here are a few guidelines to consider when you sell your
product at a luncheon:

1. Pick a restaurant that is quiet or at least has a quiet spot.
   Restaurants that have partitioned booths are ideal. Prospects fear and do not appreciate others listening in. They
   want this to be as confidential as if it were taking place in an
   office.

2. Don't be rushed and have people staring at you to hurry
   and vacate your table. If possible, make reservations for 1:00
   P.M. or 1:15 P.M., toward the end of the noon rush traffic.

3. Use your eating time to get better acquainted, asking questions, and obtaining information.

4. Order a second cup of coffee, have the dishes cleared, and
   then start your sales talk. The table is now clear for papers
   and working. You can converse without interruptions.

USE THE TELEPHONE TO FOLLOW UP A LETTER OR DIRECT MAIL. Many
salespeople like to write a short letter to the prospect before making
the phone call. Some enclose a brochure or direct mail material.
Some salespeople feel that the letter should be handwritten. I cannot say which is better, typed or handwritten, but I know a well-
thought-out letter before the phone call can be very beneficial. The
letter should be brief, should contain a mind-opening or attention-
getting statement, and then should state that you will call within a
certain period of time to set up an interview.

For example, "Mr. Jones, I've got some exciting new ideas for
you that could help you cut down reruns, get the most production
from the people on your payroll, and add some insurance that your
customers will give you even more repeat business. I will call you
within 48 hours to set up an appointment to discuss this very
important matter." Or you could be more specific and say, "I will
call Wednesday at 9:30 A.M. to set up an appointment to discuss this
very important matter."

Letters help to break the ice for the phone call, and they also supply motivation to the salesperson to make that phone call, because he or she has made a commitment to the prospect that a call will be made. Of course, when you call, mention that you are following up on the letter you sent the prospect. This mention should be made right at the start of the fourth step in the previous outline.

You should verify that the letter was received. Then, briefly repeat the mind opener or attention getter, then proceed to number 5, and then right on to number 6. If the prospect did not receive your letter, you can do one of two things: tell him or her that you will remail it and call back, or go right ahead with your telephone outline to secure the appointment.

If the prospect says, "I hear the cost of your equipment is very high. How much is it?" reply, "That's the kind of question and information I want to discuss with you in detail, face to face. Is Monday at 10:00 A.M. okay, or would Tuesday at 1:30 P.M. be better?" Again, don't fall into the trap of trying to sell the product on the phone. Just sell the interview.

KEEP SCORE. Work hard to improve your appointment-closing ratio. Believe in telephoning. When telephoning is done skillfully, it becomes an enjoyable way of scheduling effective appointments, which can lead to more sales closed. Telephoning time should be included in your overall goal plan.

Set aside X number of minutes per day for the telephone. You must also carefully analyze the best time of the day to reach your prospects.

Here is a checklist to use after a telephoning session:

1. Was my attitude positive?
2. Was I natural? Having a good time? Cheerful? Smiling?
3. Was my message easily understood?
4. Did I open the prospect's mind and talk just enough about benefits to motivate him or her to feel justified in making the appointment?
5. Did I get trapped into giving too much information?

6. Did I ask for the appointment instead of hinting at it or assuming that I wouldn't get it?

7. Was I polite? A good listener? Correct in analyzing the prospect?

8. Did I use good grammar?

9. Did I avoid trite, overworked phrases?

10. Did I give my prospect a choice of two appointment times?

11. Did I speak with complete confidence?

12. Did I pronounce the prospect's name correctly?

13. Did I qualify the prospect?

14. Did I speak to the prospect as I would like someone to speak to me on the phone?

15. Did I stay in control?

16. Did I handle the objections and stalls successfully?

SUCCESSFUL PROSPECTING LEADS TO MORE SUCCESSFUL PROSPECTING

SUCCESSFUL PROSPECTING IS THE LIFE BLOOD OF THE SUCCESSFUL SALESPERSON. Closing the sale starts right here with the first contact with the prospect. Train yourself to prospect successfully, and you will soon enjoy bigger and better commissions.

THOUGHT-PROVOKING QUOTES

A man's true delight is to do the things he was made for. He was made to show good will to his kind, to rise above the promptings of his senses, to distinguish appearances from realities, and to pursue the study of universal nature and her works.

MARCUS AURELIUS

What a man is is the basis of what he dreams and thinks, accepts and rejects, feels and perceives.

JOHN MASON BROWN

You cannot bring about prosperity by discouraging thrift.

EDWARD EVERETT HALE

Of all men's miseries, the bitterest is this, to know so much and have control over nothing.
HERODOTUS

It is well to treasure the memories of past misfortunes; they constitute our bank of fortitude.
ERIC HOFFER

Better be proficient in one art than a smatterer in a hundred.
JAPANESE PROVERB

Nature gave men two ends—one to sit on and one to think with. Ever since then man's success or failure has been dependent on the one he used most.
GEORGE R. KILPATRICK

There are no circumstances, however unfortunate, that clever people do not extract some advantage from.
LA ROCHEFOUCAULD

Keeping a little ahead of conditions is one of the secrets of business; the trailer seldom goes far.
CHARLES SCHWAB

There is no higher religion than human service. To work for the common good is the greatest creed.
ALBERT SCHWEITZER

Look for the good things, not the faults. It takes a good deal bigger-sized brain to find out what is not wrong with people and things than to find out what is wrong.
R. L. SHARPE

Opportunity is rare, and a wise man will never let it go by him.
BAYARD TAYLOR

Democracy is based on the conviction that man has the moral and intellectual capacity, as well as the inalienable right, to govern himself with reason and justice.
HARRY S. TRUMAN

Action is the last resource of those who know not how to dream.
OSCAR WILDE

chapter fourteen

SELLING CAREERS REFUSE TO BE MISMANAGED FOR LONG

Victories that are easy are cheap. Those only are worth
having which come as the result of hard fighting.
HENRY WARD BEECHER

WHEN IT'S OVER IN THE MIND, IT'S OVER

"A determined soul will do more with a rusty monkey wrench than a loafer will accomplish with all of the tools in a machine shop," said Rupert Hughes. This is also true for salespeople. You see it every day. So very many salespeople do so little with all of the tools of the trade that they have or certainly could have. What a waste of time and talent!

When a person sets out to become a professional salesperson and does not succeed, it is because he or she became convinced that it could not be done, or else he or she didn't want to do it badly enough.

A salesperson's attitude, territory, selling day—all of those important things refuse to be mismanaged for very long.

To the salesperson who mismanages his or her career, problems soon become insurmountable challenges, production goes down, depression sets in, excuses galore pop up, and then comes the often-heard phrase *sales slump*. Webster defines *slump* as "to fall, sink, or collapse." That salesperson has mentally handed in a resignation.

Many salespeople seem to enjoy being in a sales slump because they spend a great deal of time talking about it and they spend little, if any, effort attempting to get out of it. Apparently, it sounds good to them because it justifies their lack of production. No salesperson can climb out beyond the limitations of his or her own character. Plato said, "To conquer oneself is the best and noblest victory."

There's absolutely no doubt about it; when it's over in a salesperson's mind, it's over! I've heard the slump excuse from many salespeople just before they quit or terminate their jobs. I also have heard other negative remarks like, "There's no use calling on them because . . .," or "You can't sell the farmers anything; the corn crop wasn't up to par this year," or "They told me to come back in three or four months; they couldn't afford it just now," or "You'd be wasting your time calling on Jones because he was too busy to see me."

These salespeople have lost the sale in their minds. I have seen other salespeople step in and take over these sellers' territory and have good to excellent production right at the very start.

Obviously, the negative salespeople mismanaged their selling careers and they paid the price—failure. Yet, in the case of practically every failure, mismanagement was the individual's own doing. Failures blame other people and they blame things, but in the end they simply do it to themselves.

KEEP YOUR SELLING CAREER ON
THE RIGHT TRACK

THE BEST INSURANCE AGAINST MISMANAGEMENT OF YOUR SELLING CAREER IS FOR YOU TO START EACH SELLING DAY BY MENTALLY OR PHYSICALLY REVIEWING YOUR GOAL PLAN. Start each day on the right foot. Every morning review your daily, weekly, monthly, and yearly goals. I urge you to write out a very complete goal plan and include even the smallest details, leaving nothing to chance.

According to Webster, a *goal* is "the line or place at which a race, trip, etc., is ended; an object or end that one strives to attain; aim." Think about your major and sustaining goals all the time. Every person on the face of this earth becomes what he or she thinks about becoming.

THOUGHT WITHOUT ACTION IS AS USELESS AS ACTION WITHOUT THOUGHT. The salespeople who are persistent and determined to reach their major goals must follow through on their sustaining goals. They must be sure that all specific activities are accomplished. Constant thought plus action makes it become a reality. Your selling career is controlled by you—by your thinking and by your actions. Your thoughts and actions are controlled by your attitude toward your goals. I love the words of Thomas Carlyle: "Let each of us become all that we are capable of being."

Have you written out your complete, worthy goal plan in detail?

BELIEVE YOU WILL ACHIEVE YOUR WORTHY
GOALS, AND YOU WILL ACHIEVE THEM

YOU BECOME WHAT YOU BELIEVE YOURSELF TO BE. It has been proven many times over the centuries that a person becomes exactly what he or she believes himself or herself to be. Mohandas Gandhi expressed it so well when he said, "Man becomes what he believes himself to be. If I keep saying to myself that I cannot do a certain thing, it is possible that I may end up really becoming incapable of doing it. On the contrary, if I have the belief that I can do it, I shall surely acquire the capacity to do it even if I may not have it at the beginning." Self-reliance and self-respect are very valuable qualities and are essential for great accomplishments.

SELLING JOBS DON'T HAVE FUTURES; PEOPLE DO

IT ISN'T THE SIZE OF THE TERRITORY, BUT THE SIZE OF THE PERSON IN THE TERRITORY. The size of the person and his or her future is dependent upon one word that has been discussed in this book many times—*attitude.* Your attitude determines how far you will progress in the future. Jobs don't have futures; people do. Promotions, high commissions, and firings all go right back to the person on the job, not to the job itself.

GIVE POSITIVE RADIATION TO THE PROSPECT

THE RIGHT ATTITUDE WILL MAKE YOU A DYNAMIC, POWERFUL SALESPERSON. Never lose sight of the fact that your attitude, in every selling situation, sets the pace for the prospect. You control the prospect's reactions.

Your attitude, your burning enthusiasm, your true desire to serve the buyer, your integrity, your honesty, your confidence, your sincerity, and your heartfelt conviction are given off to the prospect just like the odor given off by hickory chips in the fire of a barbecue. Those qualities give you the positive radiation that makes the prospect go from cold to hot, from a prospect to a solid, well-sold customer.

Many years ago, when I was with the Union Pacific Railroad, practically every depot was heated with the old pot-bellied stoves. I can remember going to work a few minutes early to build a fire to warm up the work area. It wouldn't take long. I would build a good fire, light it, open the drafts, and before long that old pot-bellied stove was red-hot and radiating a great amount of heat, warming up the entire depot.

I compare a salesperson to that old pot-bellied stove. First, you have to build a fire inside you, a fire with all of the qualities I have discussed above. Then, you have to light it, open the drafts of enthusiasm, and, almost instantly, your positive radiation can be felt by the prospect.

You can be sure that when you have your fire burning on the inside and your stove is red-hot, you are going to melt all of the prospect's icicles and turn that cold prospect into a red-hot happy customer.

The salespeople who have that red-hot fire on the inside do not have to worry about a job or job security. They have an unlimited future!

ONLY YOUR BEST WILL DO

WORK WITH EVERYTHING YOU'VE GOT. All of the successful salespeople I have had the privilege of knowing have had one thing in common: they love what they are doing. They enjoy their work. Their work is very exciting to them. They always get a great amount of satisfaction out of meeting challenges head on. They work with everything they've got. There is no holding back. They always put their best efforts into every phase of their work.

John Burroughs said:

> Few people realize how much of their happiness is dependent upon their work, upon the fact that they are kept busy and not left to feed upon themselves. Happiness comes most to persons who seek her least and think least about it. It is not an object to be sought; it is a state to be induced. It must follow and not lead.

> It must overtake you, and not you overtake it. How important is health to happiness, yet the best promoter of health is something to do.
>
> Blessed is the man who has some congenial work, some occupation in which he can put his heart and which affords a complete outlet to all the forces there are in him.

I know that money is important to you. You have to live. You have certain family obligations and responsibilities. But the salesperson who does not work for the love of his or her work and works strictly for money is not likely to make very much money and is not going to have much fun in life.

There's so much truth in Elbert Green Hubbard's statement: "Folks who never do any more than they get paid for never get paid for any more than they do."

LOVE YOUR JOB AND PUT ALL YOU'VE GOT INTO IT. Only your best will do. It will be fun meeting your various obligations and responsibilities. You will make more money and you will be much happier.

Plato said, "The man who makes everything that leads to happiness, depends upon himself, and not upon other men, has adopted the very best plan for living happily. This is the man of moderation, the man of manly character and wisdom."

BE WARY OF WHO INFLUENCES WHOM

THE NEGATIVES DO TALK. My work clearly brings out that there are far more people who are negatives than there are those who are positives. Every reliable source I have ever heard of or read about indicates the same. Unfortunately, the majority of the people, the negatives, talk the most. Their negative conversations and remarks are constantly bombarding the fewer salespeople who are positive. Don't for one minute pay any attention to them. Don't believe the negatives. Don't let their "stinkin' thinkin' " influence you in any way.

STAY POSITIVE. Keep your mind on your goal and know that you are right. Be stronger than the negatives are. It's a test for your confidence and character. The negatives may even make fun of you, try to belittle you, and make up jokes about you, but never let them influence you!

Your payoff is this: You can enjoy every minute of your career, laugh and smile every time you make a trip to the bank to deposit your well-earned commissions.

OUT OF 100 SALESPEOPLE, 84 QUIT
WITHIN FOUR YEARS

Last evening I read an article in *Money* magazine. It started out like this: "Of every 100 new life insurance agents, 84 quit within the first four years, unable to earn enough to pay the food bills." The balance of the article was all about how one saleswoman was able to make outstanding, large commissions. This article certainly substantiated the figures I have quoted several times in this book.

DON'T TALK ABOUT IT—DO IT

TAKE COMMAND OF YOUR SELLING CAREER. Don't let it be mismanaged for one minute. Never be satisfied with anything other than your best. Don't procrastinate for one minute about putting your goal plan into positive action. Make it a point always to trust yourself. Never doubt yourself. When you doubt yourself, you lose control of yourself and your career. Not to have control over your career is like sailing a ship without a rudder—it's bound to break into pieces upon coming into contact with the very first rock.

To sum up these fourteen chapters, if you constantly remind yourself to analyze the successes and failures of each selling day and learn from both, and if you work harder and smarter each day, there is absolutely nothing that will keep you from making your goal plan become a reality.

I am closing this book with the title of my first book: "Don't talk about it—do it!"

THOUGHT-PROVOKING QUOTES

A disciplined conscience is a man's best friend. It may not be his most amiable, but it is his most faithful monitor.
HENRY WARD BEECHER

Happiness is not the end of life, character is.
HENRY WARD BEECHER

Every man is the painter and the sculptor of his own life.
SAINT JOHN CHRYSOSTOM

Team spirit is what gives so many companies an edge over their competitors.
GEORGE L. CLEMENTS

This is a world of action, and not for moping and droning in.
CHARLES DICKENS

No man can do anything well who does not esteem his work to be of importance.
RALPH WALDO EMERSON

People seem not to see that their opinion of the world is also a confession of character. We can only see what we are; if we misbehave, we suspect others.
RALPH WALDO EMERSON

If money is your hope for independence you will never have it. The only real security that a man can have in this world is a reserve of knowledge, experience, and ability.
HENRY FORD

He who enjoys doing and enjoys doing what he has done is happy.
GOETHE

So act that your principle of action might safely be made a law for the whole world.
IMMANUEL KANT

The individual has a strong desire to become himself; given a favorable psychological climate he drops the defensive masks with which he has faced life, and begins to discover and to experience the stranger who lives behind these masks—the hidden parts of himself.
CARL R. ROGERS

It is not enough to be industrious; so are the ants. What are you industrious about?
HENRY DAVID THOREAU

Envy is wanting what someone else has without knowing fully what he's got.
FRANK TYGER

179

INDEX